Downward Entailing and Chinese Polarity Items

Polarity phenomena are pervasively observed in natural languages. Previous studies on Chinese polarity items are mainly in line with the non-veridicality approach. This book, however, employs the downward-entailing hypothesis as its analytical foundation, and argues that downward entailment is the only licensor for different kinds of Chinese polarity items, and non-veridicality is neither a necessary nor sufficient condition and thus offers inferior explanatory power compared with the former.

To begin with, it lays the groundwork for this research by presenting a brief introduction to polarity phenomena and reviewing the existing relevant theories. Then it addresses the status of the commonly used element *dou* in Chinese. Specifically, it applies the tripartite structure to the studies of *dou*, and examines the role of *dou* in licensing the polarity items. Moreover, it investigates the properties and behavior of *dou* with respect to modality. Based on the analysis above, it observes that non-interrogative *wh*-indeterminates in Chinese can be licensed in the restriction domain of a necessity operator. Also, the non-uniformity of three Chinese polarity items, i.e., *shenme, na*-CL, and *renhe*, is scrutinized within the downward-entailing framework.

This book will appeal to scholars, teachers and students in the field of linguistics, especially in the areas of formal semantics and generative grammar. Researchers and engineers in cloud computing and big data who are seeking help from linguistic contributions to meaning and logic will also benefit from it.

Li Chen is an Assistant Professor in the School of Humanities, Shanghai Jiao Tong University. Her research interests lie in syntax, formal semantics and psycholinguistics.

Frontiers in Applied Linguistics
Series Editor: Kaibao Hu
Professor of Translation Studies and Dean of the School of Foreign Languages, Shanghai Jiao Tong University

Frontiers in Applied Linguistics focuses on the development of applied linguistics in the Chinese-speaking world. Although extensive researches have been carried out in the field of applied linguistics, most studies have primarily concentrated on Indo-European speakers. This series is expected to fill the void. Each volume in the series will address different issues, and strike a balance between methodological and theoretical discussion on empirical researches into applied linguistics in the Chinese context.

Titles in this series currently include

English Transitivity Alternation in Second Language Acquisition
An Attentional Approach
Yuxia Wang

Quotation and Truth-Conditional Pragmatics
Xiaofei Wang

Downward Entailing and Chinese Polarity Items
Li Chen

A Study of Academic English Genre
Xiuyun Lei

For more information about this series, please visit: www.routledge.com/Frontiers-in-Applied-Linguistics/book-series/FAL

Downward Entailing and Chinese Polarity Items

Li Chen

LONDON AND NEW YORK

First published 2018
by Routledge
2 Park Square, Milton Park, Abingdon, Oxon OX14 4RN

and by Routledge
711 Third Avenue, New York, NY 10017

Routledge is an imprint of the Taylor & Francis Group, an informa business

© 2018 Li Chen

The right of Li Chen to be identified as author of this work has been asserted by her in accordance with sections 77 and 78 of the Copyright, Designs and Patents Act 1988.

All rights reserved. No part of this book may be reprinted or reproduced or utilised in any form or by any electronic, mechanical, or other means, now known or hereafter invented, including photocopying and recording, or in any information storage or retrieval system, without permission in writing from the publishers.

Trademark notice: Product or corporate names may be trademarks or registered trademarks, and are used only for identification and explanation without intent to infringe.

British Library Cataloguing-in-Publication Data
A catalogue record for this book is available from the British Library

Library of Congress Cataloging-in-Publication Data
A catalog record has been requested for this book

ISBN: 978-1-138-57681-0 (hbk)
ISBN: 978-1-351-26884-4 (ebk)

Typeset in Times New Roman
by Apex CoVantage, LLC

Contents

	Acknowledgements	vi
	List of abbreviations	viii
	Introduction	ix
1	Polarity theories and polarity phenomena	1
2	Non-veridicality approach and the challenge from *dou* sentences	27
3	Tripartite structure and *dou*	58
4	Downward entailment approach	67
5	*Dou* as a necessity operator	85
6	The non-uniformity of Chinese polarity items	98
7	Conclusions	114
	References	117
	Index	123

Acknowledgements

This book could not have been completed without the help and support of many people, who are gratefully acknowledged here.

At the very first, I'm honored to express my deepest gratitude to my supervisor, Prof. Pan Haihua. I could not have worked out the ideas expressed in this book without his guidance and support. He has offered me valuable insight, suggestions, and criticisms with his profound knowledge of linguistics and rich research experience. He is always willing to discuss ideas with me anytime he is available – and even when he is quite busy, he spares time for me. His patience and kindness are greatly appreciated, and his wisdom has set a wonderful example for me to follow as I become a real linguist. I have learned from him a lot, not only about book writing, but also about professional practice.

I also want to express my gratitude to many teachers, colleagues, and friends in the Department of Chinese, Translation, and Linguistics at City University of Hong Kong. I'm grateful to Dr. Lee Po-lun and Prof. Hu Jianhua, whose patient and meticulous guidance and invaluable suggestions were indispensable to the completion of this book. Their strong support and encouragement gave me confidence and motivation to work out the final version of this project. I also benefited a lot from the assistance of Dr. Jiang Yan, who gave me many detailed comments and suggestions on earlier ideas related to the present book during his course. I am also grateful for Prof. Xu Liejiong, whose important comments and suggestions shed much light on my thoughts.

I wish to extend my thanks to Prof. Lu Jianming and Prof. Shen Yang, who introduced me into the world of linguistics. They are always ready to help me whenever I have difficulties and questions. Thanks also to the scholars who helped me during my studies in Hong Kong. In particular, I would like to thank Mr. Tom Lai and Dr. Gerner Matthias for helping me become a tutor and giving me insight into my future career.

I am no less indebted to my fellow students at the Department of Chinese, Translation, and Linguistics, and to all the friends who have accompanied and supported me, in particular Wang Yuxia, Liu Huijuan, Lu Shuo, Feng Yuli, Wuyun, Cui Yuzhen, Ling Feng, Zeng Li, Peng Gongguan, Liu Chong, Zhang Xin, Li Jian, and Wang Xia. Thanks to them for sharing their viewpoints and experience of study as well as life with me. I am also grateful to Caitlin Keenan and Li Fengyuan for their editorial guidance.

Special thanks to Zhou Yingbo for tolerating my ill temper during the writing of this book. I would also like to express my deepest love for my mother. She believes in me when I find it difficult to believe in myself. For her love, I feel so happy and strong wherever I go and whatever I do.

Abbreviations

DE	Downward Entailing
DW	Domain Widening
EPW	Existential Polarity *wh*-phrase
FC	Free Choice
FCI	Free Choice Items
LF	Logic Form
NEEC	Non-Entailment-of-Existence Condition
NP	Noun Phrase
NPI	Negative Polarity Item
PS	Polarity Sensitive, Polarity Sensitivity
PSI	Polarity Sensitive Item
SDE	Strawson Downward Entailing
UE	Upward Entailing
UG	Universal Grammar
VP	Verb Phrase

Introduction

Polarity phenomena are pervasively observed in natural languages. Polarity items are so-named because of their sensitivity to the negative or affirmative property of the sentences they occur in; this is known as 'polarity sensitivity'. Two main theoretical approaches have been proposed to analyze polarity phenomena cross-linguistically. First, the downward entailment approach argues that polarity items are sensitive to the monotonicity of the sentence containing them (cf. Ladusaw, 1979; Kadmon and Landman, 1993; Lahiri, 1998; Kratzer, 2005; Chierchia, 2006, among others). Second, the non-veridicality approach holds that polarity items are sensitive to the (non-)veridicality of the sentence containing them (cf. Zwarts, 1995; Lin, 1998; Giannakidou, 1998, 2001, among others).

In line with the second approach, previous studies on Chinese polarity items have treated non-veridicality as the primary polarity licensor. This approach is elaborated in Lin (1998)'s *non-entailment-of-existence condition*, Li (1992)'s *non-positively-fixed truth condition*, and a reformulation of these two pieces of work in terms of *non-veridicality* and *intensionality*, presented by Cheng and Giannakidou (2005, 2013). The present study reanalyzes the relevant Mandarin Chinese data, and compares the two major approaches and their applications in the study of Mandarin polarity phenomena. Based on this assessment, I argue for a downward entailment approach to Mandarin polarity items. I further demonstrate that non-interrogative '*shenme* NP', '*na* +CL +NP', and '*renhe* NP' are only licensed under this condition, and that non-veridicality is neither a necessary nor sufficient condition for licensing polarity items.

To rebut the non-veridicality approach, this book also scrutinizes the co-occurrence of the polarity items and dou-a common pairing in Mandarin that does not appear to be subject to the constraints of veridicality or non-veridicality. Adopting a tripartite structure account as an analytical tool, this book treats dou as a universal quantifier that introduces a tripartite structure along the lines proposed by Pan (2006). Under this approach, all the various interpretations of dou receive a unified account; the differences between them are reflected in the diverse mapping mechanisms that can apply between the sentence components themselves and the structural configuration of the tripartite structure's restriction domain and nuclear scope. The downward-entailing property of the restriction domain of dou's tripartite structure allows the co-occurrence of dou and polarity items to be accounted for by the licensing power of downward entailment. The analysis I adopt allows us to attribute this particular linguistic phenomenon in Mandarin to the scope of universal grammar, while also providing strong support for the downward entailment approach to polarity items.

It has long been observed that one function of polarity items is domain widening, which induces a maximal domain in NP so that the resulting DP can only be licensed in a downward-entailing environment (Kadmon and Landman, 1993; Chierchia, 2006). In this book, I argue that downward entailment itself is not assessed on the surface level or any other linguistic level, but with respect to the restriction domain of the relevant tripartite structure on which domain widening relies. I show that this account is simpler and has more extensive explanatory power than an earlier analysis by von Fintel (1999), and thus successfully rescues the downward entailment approach.

Last but not least, in this book, I scrutinize and account for the different behavior of the various Chinese polarity items within the downward entailment framework. Concentrating on the different morphological structures of *renhe* and *shenme*, I propose that *renhe*, as a universal quantifier, is used as a free-choice item, while *shenme*, as an existential quantifier, is used as a negative polarity item. I argue that the different behavior of *shenme* and *na*-CL polarity items is a result of the (non-)D-linking property they have. D-linked *na*-CL presupposes a non-empty given set and prefers a sentence-initial position, while non-D-linked *shenme* does the opposite.

1 Polarity theories and polarity phenomena

The main goal of my research program is to investigate Chinese polarity sensitivity and determine which of the two major approaches to polarity (the non-veridicality approach and the downward entailment approach) is most applicable to the Mandarin Chinese data. In this chapter, I will lay the groundwork for this research by presenting a brief introduction to polarity phenomena and provide an overview of existing theories about polarity sensitivity. The following theories will be discussed:

1   the original theory by Klima (1964), who invented the term 'affectivity' and inspired subsequent researchers profoundly;
2   the well-known account of polarity sensitivity in downward entailment contexts proposed by Ladusaw (1979), whose work made the theories on polarity valuable and logically reasonable, as this book will show them to be;
3   the domain-widening approach conceived by Kadmon and Landman (1993), who made further efforts to explain why polarity items are sensitive to downward entailment contexts;
4   various morphological perspectives on *even* as the lexical source of polarity sensitivity, including Lee and Horn (1994) and Lahiri (1998);
5   Giannakidou's (1997 and following) non-veridicality proposal, which unified polarity licensors as a class; this approach is also broadly consistent with studies on Chinese polarity phenomena.

In addition to these theoretical works on polarity, I will present an empirical approach to the problem: Krifka's typological classification of polarity items.

After considering the universal aspects of polarity phenomena and summarizing these theories on polarity sensitivity, I will review previous studies on Chinese polarity items. The majority of current polarity theories only address English data, with a particular focus on the word *any*; however, researchers have also investigated the non-interrogative use of Mandarin *wh*-elements (also called *wh*-indefinites, *wh*-indeterminates, or *wh*-polarity items) and the polarity usage of Mandarin *renhe*, which is somewhat parallel to *any* in English.

1.1 Polarity phenomena

Polarity phenomena are pervasive in nature language, and negative polarity items (NPIs) are typologically very common (for instance, Haspelmath, 1997 reported evidence of NPIs from 40 languages). One of the hallmark properties of NPIs is their inability to occur in positive episodic sentences (Giannakidou, 1997). English *any* (first identified in Klima's, 1964 work on English negation), Greek *tipota*, and Dutch *ook maar iets* are all well-known NPIs:

(1) a   Bill didn't buy any books.   English
    b   * Bill bought **any** books.
(2) a   Dhen idhe tipota o Janis.   Greek
       not saw anything the John
       John didn't see anything.
    b   * Idhe **tipota** o Janis.
       nobody has *even* something seen
       Nobody saw anything.
(3) a   Niemand heeft ook maar iets gezien.   Dutch
       nobody has even something seen
       Nobody saw anything.
    b   * Jan heeft **ook maar iets** gezien.
       * John saw anything.
(4) a   2012 nian shou jidu mei fasheng shenme dongluan.   Mandarin
       2012 year first quarter not happen what trouble
       There is not any trouble that broke out during the first quarter of 2012.
    b   * 2012 nian shou jidu fasheng le shenme dongluan.
       2012 year first quarter happen le what trouble
       * There is any trouble that broke out during the first quarter of 2012.

These examples from English, Greek, Dutch and Mandarin simply illustrate the polarity phenomenon. Numerous polarity theories have been developed that explore this phenomenon in more depth. As we shall see, this is one of those pleasing areas of linguistics where the phenomenon drives the theory to develop and the theory, in turn, helps the phenomenon to be understood more deeply. In the next section, I describe several of the most prominent of these theories.

1.2 Polarity theories

1.2.1 Affectivity as an original concept

Theories of polarity sensitivity can be divided into two major traditional camps, one focused on syntax and the other on semantics. Both of these perspectives find their roots in Klima's work *Negation in English*. Klima (1964) clearly distinguished two basic questions (cf. Ladusaw, 1996): (i) what makes something a polarity licensor?; and (ii) what sort of relation must obtain for a licensor to license a polarity item? Klima proposed that polarity licensors share a 'grammatico-semantic property' that he called affectivity, and that NPIs are licensed if they occur 'in construction with' ('are c-commanded by', in later terminology) an appropriately affective licensor. Licensors are either an overt negation or an affective element, e.g., a verb like *surprised*.

(5) a   John didn't say anything.
     b   We were surprised that John said anything.

These two questions identified by Klima have guided most modern accounts of polarity: semantic theories, in general, focus on the problem of how to elaborate the notion of affectivity (Heim, 1984; Kadmon and Landman, 1993; Kas, 1993; Dowty, 1994; Zwarts, 1995; Giannakidou, 1998); syntactic accounts, on the other hand, focus less on the variety of licensors and more on the syntactic relations that must hold between a licensor (usually negation) and a licensed polarity item (Laka, 1990; Progovac, 1993, 1994; Kato, 2000). Next, some typical theories will be reviewed in turn.

1.2.2 Downward-entailing hypothesis

NPIs are defined by their distribution and close relationship to negation. Building on Klima's notion of affectivity, Fauconnier (1975) and Ladusaw (1979) employed the idea of downward entailment to successfully capture the occurrence of NPIs in certain apparently non-negative environments. This was a remarkable achievement, and the downward-entailing approach initiated a fruitful research program for semanticists (Zwarts, 1993, 1995; Kas, 1993; Dowty, 1994; Wouden, 1997; Lahiri, 1998; Hoeksema, 2000, among many others). Specifically, Ladusaw proposed that NPIs are sensitive to logical monotonicity, and can only be licensed in the scope of a downward-entailing operator. The downward-entailing operator and upward-entailing operator are defined as follows:

(6) Op is upward entailing iff for every X,Y: if $X \leq Y$, then $Op(X) \leq Op(Y)$;
(7) Op is downward entailing iff for every X,Y: if $X \leq Y$, then $Op(Y) \leq Op(X)$.

Intuitively, a downward-entailing context licenses inferences from general properties to specific instances, from sets to subsets. Negation is a downward-entailing operator because it allows inferences as in (8): from the general, *a bird*, to the specific, *a penguin*.

(8) a   Beth didn't see a bird in the garden.   → (entails)
     b   Beth didn't see a penguin in the garden.

Upward-entailing (UE) contexts (for example, simple affirmatives) license inferences in the other direction, from specific instances to general cases, as the contrast between (9) and (10) shows.

(9) a   Beth saw a bird in the garden. $\neq\rightarrow$
     b   Beth saw a penguin in the garden.

4 *Polarity theories and polarity phenomena*

(10) a   Beth saw a penguin in the garden. →
     b   Beth saw a bird in the garden.

According to Ladusaw, whether the following four sentences in (11) and (12) are grammatical depends on whether *any* appears within the scope of a downward-entailing operator:

(11) a   I don't have any potatoes.
     b   * I have *any* potatoes.
(12) a   Few of the books had any readers.
     b   * Many of the books had *any* readers.

The two (a) sentences above are grammatical, because in each case *any* occurs within the scope of a downward-entailing operator: the negation in (11a) and *few of the books* in (12a); conversely, the (b) sentences are ungrammatical because *any* is not in the scope of a downward-entailing operator. One advantage of Ladusaw's semantic theory is that it captures the occurrence of NPIs (like 'student who likes linguistics' in (13)) in the restriction of *every*, an environment that had nothing to do with negation.

(13) a   Every [student who likes linguistics] came to the party. →
     b   Every student who likes syntax came to the party.

Although the formal prediction of Ladusaw's theory (NPIs are licit in the scope of a downward-entailing operator) can be viewed as one of its advantages, some data also suggest that the downward-entailing condition is not sufficient. It does not predict all the correct licensing environments; for example, downward entailment cannot explain the occurrence of NPIs in questions (Giannakidou, 2008). It is very hard to establish monotonicity patterns in an interrogative environment, yet NPIs are very common in questions. Han and Laura (1996) helped to solve this problem by arguing that in real *wh*-questions and *yes – no* questions, covert negation is derived from the semantics, and it is this covert negation that licenses the NPIs.

Szabolcsi, Bott and Mcelree (2008), however, show that the facilitator role of NPIs in inference making is not unproblematic. The authors conducted three groups of experiments and reported that the presence of an NPI does not facilitate the processing of the inference from set to subset, as expected. In fact, the most straightforward implication of Szabolcsi and colleagues' experimental work is the most unexpected: the processor does not recognize the close relationship between NPIs and downward-entailing contexts! This finding directly contradicts the general premise that downward-entailing operators are the semantic licensors of NPIs. As I will show in the chapters that follow, however, it may not be necessary for processors to intuitively recognize the relationship between NPIs and downward-entailing contexts, even when a downward-entailing operator is the semantic licensor of an NPI.

The downward-entailing approach to polar sensitivity has continued to receive a great deal of attention in the literature, with researchers variously challenging or defending it. For example, Gajewski (2010) points out that the ability of the English determiner *most* to license NPIs has long stood as a puzzle for theories that follow Ladusaw (1979) in claiming that NPIs must appear in the scope of downward-entailing operators. *Most* licenses NPIs such as *any* and *ever* in its restrictor despite not being downward (or upward) entailing with respect to its restrictor. Gajewski (2010) argues that, despite appearances to the contrary, NPIs in the restrictor of *most* are in the scope of a downward-entailing operator. Gajewski makes crucial use of a recent proposal by Hackl (2009) to compositionally analyze the determiner *most* as a superlative expression. When the semantics of the superlative morpheme are spelled out correctly, it is possible to derive the result that *most* licenses NPIs in its restrictor. In addition, Gajewski (2010) shows that this approach correctly predicts the NPI-licensing properties of relative *most*, as in *the most students*.

In this book, I will consider the question of why polarity items can be licensed in sentences with *only* – a problem for the downward-entailing hypobook of negative polarity licensing. This phenomenon occurs not only in English, but also in German, Dutch and Spanish (where VP-modifying exclusives license NPIs in non-focal material), as Beaver and Clark (2008) show. In this book, I will add Mandarin Chinese *dou* to the list of *only*-like elements, arguing that *dou* behaves like *only* in terms of its licensing behavior with polarity items.

1.2.3 Domain-widening hypothesis

Not only did the downward-entailing approach provide an important foundation for much subsequent research into polarity items, but it also introduced a new question: why are NPIs used in monotone-decreasing contexts? What function does the presence of an NPI in these contexts serve? It was Kadmon and Landman (1993) who first put forth a proposal to answer this question: the domain-widening (DW) hypothesis. Kadmon and Landman proposed that NPIs are indefinite expressions that indicate to the hearer that he or she should consider the domain of the individual governed by the NPI to be broader than would otherwise be expected. This same notion of domain-widening allowed the authors to present a unified theory of negative polarity *any* and free choice *any*, as (14) and (15) show:

(14) Meaning of *any*
any + common noun denotes the corresponding indefinite NP or common noun, together with the additional semantic/pragmatic characteristics (widening, strengthening) contributed by *any*.

(15) Widening of *any*
In an NP of the form *any* + common noun, *any* widens the interpretation of the common noun phrase along some contextual dimension.

According to Kadmon and Landman's proposal, NPIs are indefinite expressions, with core semantics similar to other indefinite determiners such as *some* or *a(n)*. However, NPIs also carry an addition semantics not borne by other indefinites: an instruction to broaden the interpretive domain of the individuals that fall under the scope of the NPI.

(16) a   a/some student$_D$
     b   any student$_{D+}$
         where $D \subseteq D+$

Say, for instance, that the use of a plain indefinite *a/some student* naturally leads the hearer to focus on some salient domain D (say, the students around here). Uttered in the same context, the NPI expression *any student* invites the hearer to consider a set possibly larger than D along some relevant dimension, with the inclusion of cases that might otherwise have been considered marginal (visiting students, students on leave, or other peripheral cases). Here is another example:

(17) a   I don't have potatoes.
     b   I don't have *any* potatoes.

Assuming that a 'cooking/non-cooking' dimension is the relevant context for the statements in (17), (17a) conveys that the speaker has no regular potatoes (such as one might reasonably expect to use in cooking), while (17b) may indicate that the speaker has broadened his or her domain to deny possession of all possible potatoes, including marginal potatoes, such as rotten potatoes, that aren't valid in the cooking context.

Based on this domain-widening hypothesis, Kadmon and Landman present a formal account of the licensing environment of *any*. To flesh out their account, the authors argue that *any* doesn't just widen the domain of the nominal element in its scope, but also carries a strengthening connotation. In other words, the domain-widening effect of *any* must have a special purpose: it must make a stronger statement. Thus, NPI *any* is only licit if the statement on the wide interpretation entails the statement on the narrow interpretation. Adding this extra stipulation allows Kadmon and Landman to account for why NPIs are limited to downward-entailing contexts such as negation: after all, it's only in such contexts that widening the domain of an indefinite leads to a stronger statement. Looking back at (17), for example, we can see that (17b), 'I don't have any potatoes,' entails (17a), 'I don't have potatoes.' In a positive sentence, by contrast, widening creates a weaker statement. In this way, the grammaticality contrast between (18a) and (18b) below is accounted for. The affirmative sentence in (18b) is not licit because it does not satisfy the strengthen restriction on the use of NPIs.

(18) a   I don't have any potatoes.
     b   *I have *any* potatoes.

As Chierchia (2006) puts it, domain widening in positive sentences is 'pointless'. That is, just because it is true that I have potatoes in a widened domain, it is not necessarily true that I have potatoes in a narrower domain. For instance, I might have rotten potatoes (wide domain), but not any nice potatoes that are actually suitable for cooking. Thus, the widened statement is too weak and not very informative. In contrast, an ordinary indefinite like *potatoes* that does not induce domain widening can occur in both negative and affirmative sentences, as shown below.

(19) a   I don't have potatoes.
     b   I have potatoes.

Kadmon and Landman (1993) take their analysis a step further by applying their analysis of negative polarity *any* to free choice *any*. According to the authors, both types of *any*, free choice *any* and negative polarity *any*, can induce domain widening. In the following example, we can see this illustrated. Consider the following indefinite contrast (*an* versus *any*) along a 'health/sick' dimension.

(20) a   An owl hunts mice.
     b   *Any* owl hunts mice.

Example (20a) says that, in general, owls hunt mice. (20b) forces a broader interpretation of the domain of the owls, yielding an interpretation along the lines of 'every owl, which includes healthy and sick owls, hunts mice'. Free choice *any* here is a generic indefinite located in the restriction of the generic operator, which can be roughly understood as a universal quantifier whose restrictor is a downward-entailing context (if every student that likes semantics knows Montague, then every student that likes linguistics knows Montague). Thus, widening the domain – i.e., widening the restriction of the generic operator – creates a stronger statement in (20b) than in (20a). The sentence with the polarity sensitivity item is assigned the strongest implicature that can be factored in without contradiction. Hence, the free choice use of *any* is licensed in a generic sentence.

As we have seen, in attempting to account for the grammatical conditions to which domain widening may be linked, Kadmon and Landman (1993) stipulate (i) that domain widening is part of the lexical meaning of *any*, and (ii) that there is a semantic/pragmatic constraint that limits domain widening to occur only in contexts where it leads to strengthening. However, not all NPI researchers have taken the same approach. Krifka (1995), for instance, links domain widening directly to quantity implicatures. According to this work, an NPI activates alternatives with smaller domains, which in turn triggers an implicature that the alternative selected is the strongest for which the speaker has evidence. Yet another approach comes from Lahiri (1998), who proposes that the alternatives associated with NPIs play a role similar to the role played by focus alternatives in focus semantics (cf. Rooth, 1985). Under this analysis, the lexical meaning of NPIs has an interpretation resembling the meaning of focus particle items such as English *even*.

8   *Polarity theories and polarity phenomena*

The key idea of Chierchia (2006) is the same idea that underpins the domain-widening hypobook of Kadmon and Landman and the strengthening hypobook of Krifka. Chierchia offers two main contributions to the study of NPIs. First, he posits that domain widening can offer a unitary analysis of the two types of polarity items. Second, he proposes to understand polarity sensitivity phenomena within the system of scalar implicature. On his account, NPIs and free-choice items (FCIs) – together, known as polarity sensitivity items (PSIs) – are assumed to obligatorily induce domain widening, which can take place along two dimensions: a quantitative dimension and a qualitative dimension. Quantitatively, PSIs pick the largest possible quantificational domain among the reasonable alternative domains. In other words, the presence of a PSI forces the interpretation of the noun phrase in its scope to include 'all entities that for all we know might exist'. Qualitatively, PSIs also capture within their domain some marginal, uncertain members as well. For example, through the semantics of widening, *any owls* can wind up including in its denotation sick owls that are so far from the owl archetype that the speaker is no longer sure that they even belong to the set of 'being owls'. Chierchia also argued that FCIs and NPIs both induce domain widening; however, these two types of polarity items behave differently from each other in the ways that they induce domain widening, as we shall see.

1.2.4   Even as part of the lexical meaning of PSIs

The analysis of Kadmon and Landman (1993), discussed in the previous subsection, is one of the two major unified approaches to *any* – 'unified' in the sense that it accounts for both the negative polarity interpretation of *any* and the free-choice interpretation. Recall the major salient characteristics of Kadmon and Landman's analysis: an NP of the form *any* + common noun has the semantics of the corresponding indefinite *a* + common noun, plus the additional semantic/pragmatic characteristics of widening and strengthening contributed by *any*.

The other major unified approach to the treatment of *any* is set forward by Lee and Horn (1994). According to these authors, *any* is an indefinite expression that incorporates the semantics of the scalar focus particle *even*. This analysis is part of a family of analyses that regards *any* (and NPIs generally) as referring to the extreme value on some scale; other researchers who take a similar approach to *any* (and PSIs in general) include Krifka (1995) and Lahiri (1998). Before we dig into the details of this analysis, let's take a look at the scalar focus sensitivity of the English particle *even*.

According to Rooth (1985), the focus particle *even* triggers two presuppositions: a scalar presupposition (ScalarP) and an existential presupposition (ExistP). Consider the occurrence of *even* in different positions in the same sentence in (21) below. The presuppositions that *even* imparts to the sentence depend on the focus position with which *even* is associated:

(21) a   John even introduced [MARY] $_F$ to Bill.
     b   John *even* introduced Mary to [BILL] $_F$.

Let's consider (21a) first. This sentence conveys that Mary is the least likely person for John to introduce to Bill (ScalarP), and that there is someone other than Mary that John introduced to Bill as well (ExistP). The existential presupposition comes about due to focus, and the same effect can be observed with other focus additive particles, such as *too* and *also*; the low scalarity presupposition, however, is a unique contribution of *even* (Horn, 1989). The phrase with *even* picks out the least likely individual from a given set of alternatives. 'Likelihood' here is understood as a possibility scale, in the sense of Horn (1972, 1989). When combined with the lowest item on the possibility hierarchy in a positive sentence, the low likelihood property of *even* will yield oddity, if not totally ungrammaticality.

Lahiri (1998) explored the use of PSIs in Hindi and argued that polarity sensitivity in that language comes from the Hindi *even*-like item, *bhii* 'also, even'. In Hindi, PSIs can be formed by combining indefinites like *er* 'one' or *koii* 'someone' with the overt *even*-like item *bhii*. The morphology of PSIs in Hindi is illustrated in Table 1.1.

(22)

Table 1.1

A	er bhii = '*any, even* one'	Er 'one' + bhii 'also, even'
B	koii bhii = 'anyone, *any* (count)'	koii 'some (count)' + bhii 'also, even'
C	kuch bhii = 'anything, *any* (mass)'	kuch 'some (mass)' + bhii 'also, even
D	zaraa bhii = '*even* a little'	zarra 'little' + bhii 'also, even'

Lahiri (1998) argued that the low likelihood presupposition of *bhii* creates a conflict when combined with ONE in a positive sentence. In the following sentence, (23), for example, the co-occurrence of *even* and *one* seems odd.

(23) a   # Even ONE student arrived.
   b   #∃n [n ≠ one ∧ n students arrived] ∧∀n [n ≠ one →likelihood (n students arriving) > likelihood (one student arriving)]
   c   *Even* ONE student did not arrive.

Even in sentence (23a) should theoretically be acceptable when the condition given by (23b) is met. However, as the sign # marks, this required condition sounds strange and cannot be properly satisfied. As a result, *even* is odd in (a). We can understand the interpretive problem intuitively: since the cardinal number *one* is entailed by every other cardinal number, it is more likely that (at least) one student came, not less likely. As a result, *even one* in positive sentences will always be problematic. With negation, on the other hand, *even one* will be acceptable, because, according to Lahiri (1998), *even* scopes out of negation and yields the correct presupposition. Thus, Hindi NPIs are licensed in downward-entailing contexts.

Lee and Horn (1994) applied the morphological approach to *even* sketched earlier to both types of *any* (negative polarity and free choice). Specifically, they argued that there is a hidden *even* in both negative polarity and free choice *any*.

Thus, on their analysis, negative polarity *any* is an existential indefinite plus *even*, which presupposes a quantity scale; the scalar presupposition of negative polarity *any* carries the meaning *an X, even a single one*. Free choice *any*, on the other hand, is equivalent to a generic indefinite plus *even*. Since free choice *any* is a generic indefinite, the incorporated *even* in this expression presupposes a kind scale, carrying the meaning *an X, even + superlative*. The quantity scale induced by negative polarity *any* and the kind scale induced by free choice *any* are illustrated in (24) and (25), respectively.

(24) There isn't any boy running around in the garden.
   = There isn't even a single boy running around in the garden.
   ≠*There is not even the liveliest boy running around in the garden.
(25) Any owl hunts mice.
   ≠*Even a single owl hunts mice.
   = Even the weakest owl hunts mice.

According to Lee and Horn's (1994) analysis, *any* can occur in a sentence where either a quantity or a kind scale, associated with an indefinite, can be constructed. Thus, if we look at (26), we can see that its ungrammaticality is due to the fact that neither of these types of scales (quantity or kind) can be induced by *any* in (26a). *Any boy* cannot be replaced by *even a single boy* or *even the least active boy*. Similarly, (27) is out because neither a quantity scale nor a kind scale can be constructed for this context.

(26) a   * There is any boy running around in the garden.
     b   * There is *even* a single boy running around in the garden.
     c   * There is *even* the least active boy running around in the garden.
(27) a   * Any boy must have made this mess.
     b   * *Even* a single boy must have made this mess.
     c   * *Even* the tidiest boy must have made this mess.

1.2.5 Non-veridicality as an NPI licenser

Veridicality and non-veridicality are concepts that entered linguistics from the philosophy literature, beginning with the work of Montague (1969) and colleagues. Veridicality has a close relationship with truth value and sometimes existence. The pair of English verbs *look for* and *see* provide a good illustration of this idea. The verb *see* is veridical because of a truth-conditional entailment it carries: if *I see a unicorn* is true, then it must be true that unicorns exist. Conversely, the verb *look for* is non-veridical because it lacks this truth-conditional entailment: just because *I am looking for a unicorn* is true, it need not necessarily be true that unicorns exist.

Giannakidou (1994 and following) and Zwarts (1995) propose that polarity items are excluded from veridical sentences but are allowed in non-veridical ones, based on the following formalized definition of veridicality and non-veridicality:

(28) (Non-)veridicality for propositional operators (Giannakidou, 2006)

   I A propositional operator F is veridical iff Fp entails or presupposes that p is true in some individual's epistemic model $M_E(x)$; otherwise F is non-veridical.
   II A non-veridical operator F is anti-veridical iff Fp entails that not-p is true in some individual's epistemic model: Fp $\rightarrow \neg$ p in some $M_E(x)$.

To describe this more specifically, veridicality is a property of sentence embedding functions: a function F is veridical if Fp entails or presupposes the truth of p. If inference to the truth of p under F is not possible, F is non-veridical; non-veridicality thus captures a state of unknown (or as yet undefined) truth value. Veridicality and non-veridicality thus replace the traditional characterizations of realis (veridical) and irrealis (non-veridical). Within the class of non-veridical expressions, negation is further identified as anti-veridical, in that **not** p entails p is false.

In the definition above, Giannakidou uses a multi-model system where the truth of a proposition is evaluated with respect to an individual's epistemic model, $M_E(x)$. $M_E(x)$ is a set of worlds representing the epistemic status of the individual x; Giannakidou (1997, 1998, 1999) argues that relativization of $M_E(x)$ to a specific individual is necessary to explain a contrast among propositional attitudes in NPI licensing and mood selection.

Most previous studies on Chinese polarity items seem to follow or coincide with Giannakidou's (non-)veridicality analysis. In the later chapters of this book, I will provide criticism of this approach based on Mandarin Chinese data.

1.2.6 Summary of polarity theories

In the previous subsections, I presented an overview of the two main schools of thought concerning polarity sensitivity. The two major approaches, and their proponents, can be summarized as follows:

- **DE (downward entailment) approach** (Ladusaw, 1979; Kadmon and Landman, 1993; Krifka, 1995; Horn, 1999; Lahiri, 1998; Chierchia, 2006, 2013): polarity items are sensitive to the monotonicity of the sentence containing them.
- **Non-veridicality approach** (Li, 1992; Zwart, 1995; Lin, 1998; Giannakidou, 2001; Cheng and Giannakidou, 2005, 2013): polarity items are sensitive to the veridicality of the sentence containing them.

Historically, research on Chinese polarity items has largely been consistent with the non-veridicality approach of Giannakidou and Zwarts. In particular, two major works on Chinese NPIs both understand non-veridicality to the factor determining the licensing of polarity items:

- Lin's (1998) *non-entailment-of-existence condition*
- Li's (1992) *non-positively-fixed truth condition*

The generalizations for Mandarin Chinese first established in Lin's and Li's work were reformulated by Cheng and Giannakidou (2005, 2013) in terms of non-veridicality and intensionality. Before describing these studies on Chinese NPIs and FCIs in detail, I will first introduce the types of polarity items described by Krifka (1995).

1.2.7 Types of polarity items

Krifka (1995) descries four distinct groups of polarity items in English: expressions of a general nature, operators that widen the applicability of a predicate, referentially non-specific expressions and expressions that denote particularly small or large entities. He also provides relevant examples of each type. Although Krifka's classification and description is based on English data, it still provides an important framework for the exploration of cross-linguistic data on polarity.

- **I** **expressions of a general nature**: *any girl, any student*
- **II** **operators that widen the applicability of a predicate**: *much of a, at all* or *in the least*

    (29) a   Mary isn't much of a clarinetist.
         b   * Mary is much of a clarinetist.
    (30) a   John isn't tired at all.
         b   * John is tired at all.

- **III** **referentially non-specific expressions**: *ever*

    (31) a   Mary hasn't ever been to China.
         b   * Mary has ever been to China.

- **IV** **expressions that denote particularly small or large entities**: *a drop, a syllable, a red cent*

    (32) a   John didn't drink a drop (of alcohol) for two days.
         b   Mary didn't utter {a word/a syllable}.
         c   John doesn't have a red cent.

Three of these four groups of English polarity items generalized by Krifka find their counterparts in Mandarin Chinese. Here is an incomplete list of similar expressions in Mandarin:

- **I** **expressions of a general nature**: *renhe NP*, *wh*-indefinites (*shenme NP, na-CL etc.*)

Mandarin *wh*-indefinites are similar to Krifka's English expressions in this category in that they all express some kind of general or common nature.

II **referentially non-specific expressions**: *conglai* 'ever', *xianglai* 'ever'

(33) a   ta conglai mei qu guo zhongguo.
        he ever not go guo China.
        he has never been to China.
    b   * ta conglai qu guo zhongguo.
        he ever not go guo China.
        Intended: 'he has ever been to China.'

III **expressions that denote particularly small or large entities**: *fenhao* and *yiming* (both of which mean roughly 'one cent').

(34) a   fen-hao-bi-cha 'Not a little difference'
    b   yi-wen-bu-ming 'with no money at all'

I will discuss this class of polarity items in detail in 2.5.1.4, and argue that these four-syllable frozen idioms are derived from *lian* ... *dou* ... sentences (with minimizers situated between *lian* and *dou*). Specifically, I will suggest that the end-of-scale property of minimizers matches precisely the function of the *lian* ... *dou* ... construction. The focus element must come before *dou*, which in turn introduces a set of ordered alternatives that must be at the extreme (top or bottom) of some hierarchy.

1.3 Free-choice items and negative polarity items

1.3.1 Outline of the two types of polarity items

As I alluded to in section 1.1 above, NPIs are not the only type of items that are sensitive to polarity. FCIs also fit this bill. In the opinion of Chierchia (2006), the end of the 20th and beginning of the 21st centuries have seen substantial progress in our understanding of the semantics of NPIs. During the same period, there have also been important steps forward in the analysis of FCIs. These two types of PSIs have a deep connection with each other. For instance, Haspelmath (1997) reports that among the approximately 150 languages he surveyed, roughly half of them use the same items to express negative polarity and free-choice indefinites, while the other half use different items for these two functions.

Among the many world languages that use only one item for negative polarity and free choice, English has been most thoroughly explored. Scholars generally consider that English *any* has dual quantificational force (i.e., an operator $\exists$ vs. an operator $\forall$) and restricted licensing environments. On its NPI use, as shown in (35) and (36), *any* is interpreted existentially. On its FCI use, however, it seems to have universal force, as shown in (37) and (38).

(35)   I didn't pick any card   Negation
(36)   If you pick any card, you will win the game   If-conditional
(37)   Any owl hunts mice   Generic
(38)   You can pick any card   Modal

Horn (2000) provides a thorough summary of existing scholarship on the two uses of *any*. Here, I extract a couple of key passages from his synopsis:

> In a century and a half since Hamilton and De Morgan initiated the debate a number of scholars have lined up with the former in seeing *any* as an unambiguous universal operator taking relentlessly wide scope with respect to a negative or modal trigger. This is the position codified by Reichenbach (1947), Kroch (1972), LeGrand (1975), and Eisner (1994).... Others, taking their cue from Klima (1964), Horn (1972), and Fauconnier (1975, 1979) et al. supporting the existential (or at least non-universal) status of NPI *any*, have essentially adopted De Morgan's two-*any* approach. This group includes, inter alia, Ladusaw (1979), Carlson (1980, 1981), and Linebarger (1981).
>
> (Horn, 2000, p. 160)

Rather than adopting the traditional approach to *any* as a universal and/or existential quantifier, Horn (2000) instead supports the revisionist approach initiated by Vendler and carried forward by Fauconnier, Sommers, Haspelmath, Kadmon and Landman and Jennings, according to which *any* is analyzed as a non-specific indefinite involving scalar end-points, widening and/or indiscriminacy. Rebutting various remarks in the literature stressing the typological tendency to distinguish free choice from negative polarity items (including his 1972 paper on the subject), Horn argues that the two constructions may be formally similar without being identical.

Haspelmath (1997) observed that 12 of the 40 languages that use the same form for NPIs and FCIs do contain any-like operators that are used in both free-choice and overtly negative contexts. As Horn argued, the two constructions may be formally similar without being identical. Consider Lee's (1996) view on polarity sensitivity data from Japanese, in which he distinguishes the NPI indefinite *amu+CN-to* from the FCI indeterminate *amu+CN-i-ra-to*. The latter is of clausal origin and typically occurs in overtly modal contexts:

(39) Amu chinkwu-to an o-ass-ta
 Any friend-even NEG come-PAST-DEC
 'no [not *any*] friend left.'
(40) Amu ton-i-ra-to coh-ta
 Any money-be-DEC-even O.K. – DEC
 '*any* money (whatsoever) is OK.'

C. Lee points out that both constructions contain the 'any' determiner *amu* as well as the concessive 'even' morpheme, very much in the spirit of the end-of-scale indefinite analyses of Fauconnier (1975), Lee and Horn (1994), and Israel (1996, 2004). He also stresses the role of 'the notion of arbitrary choice' in both types of *amu* constructions.

Chinese, like Japanese, contains *any*-like elements that are frequently used with both free-choice and negative polarity items. Ding et al. (1961) distinguished two such elements, both of which are *wh*-indefinites: *renzhi*, which carries a denotation roughly equal to universal quantificational force, and *xuzhi*, which carries a denotation roughly equal to existential quantificational force. Identifying and defining the real licensing conditions of these *wh*-indefinites is the most important goal of this study.

According to Horn, the relationship between negative polarity and free-choice *any* is equivalent to the relationship between the ordinary and generic indefinite end-of-scale determiner (*any* + common noun) and quantifier (*anyone, anything*, etc.). Just as non-scalar generic indefinites (*a tiger eats meat*) are related but not identical to non-scalar ordinary indefinites (*a tiger is in the garden*), so too are polarity sensitive and free-choice *any* closely related but not identical.

1.3.2 Licensing environments for the two types of polarity items

Free-choice and negative polarity *any* do not share precisely the same set of licensing environments. As we have seen above, negative polarity *any* is known to occur in downward-entailment contexts, including under the scope of negation and in the antecedent of a conditional, as in (35) and (36) (Ladusaw, 1979). By contrast, free-choice *any*, which has a universal quantification interpretation, prefers generic contexts like (37) and some modal statements like (38) (Carlson, 1980; Dayal, 1998).

In order to determine which of these two positions is the more sustainable, we rely on diagnostic evidence for the two *any*s. One famous test environment for *any* involves the *absolutely* diagnostic. According to Horn (2000), *absolutely* selects strong scalar values in general and universals in particular, as shown in (41). In (42), we can see that free-choice *any* aligns with universal reading, while negative polarity *any* aligns with the existential reading:

(41) a Absolutely {everybody/nobody/*somebody} can win.
 b Absolutely {all/none/*some/*many/*few} of them can go.
 c It's absolutely {necessary/certain/impossible/*possible/*likely}.
 d You absolutely {must/can't/mustn't/*may/*can} go.
 e She absolutely {always/never/*sometimes/*often/*seldom/*not always} eats meat.
(42) a Absolutely anyone can cook Peking duck.
   Can absolutely anybody swim the Channel? (FC *any* reading only)
 b *Kim didn't see absolutely anyone.
   *Did John see absolutely anyone?
   *If absolutely anyone leaves, Sam will commit suicide.

These examples all illustrate a well-known diagnostic favoring free-choice *any*: *almost* (along with such relatives as *nearly, absolutely*) can modify universal operators, but not existential or other non-universal operators – and, as expected, it cannot occur with negative polarity *any*. Consider the modal sentence in (43): here, free-choice *any* can be modified by *almost*, but NPI *any* cannot.

(43) a   Almost any student could ask that question.
      b   *I don't have **almost** *any* potatoes.

Dayal (1998) argued that the two forms of *any* we have seen in these examples are actually distinct, albeit related, lexical items: a free-choice *any* that is universal and a polarity sensitive *any* that is indefinite. The two items have distinct quantificational forces, yet are still similar in that they express generalizations about a class of entities rather than about particular members of the class. In that sense, both *any*s encode a kind of inherent epistemic modality internal to the noun phrase.

In this book, I do not distinguish Chinese NPIs from Chinese FCIs; rather, in most cases, I regard all Chinese polarity items as a single class. The justification for this decision, which I will illustrate at length in the chapters that follow, is the fact that the licensing conditions for the two types of Chinese polarity items do not show significant differences in behavior or distribution.

Below, I will argue that the two types of Chinese polarity items share the same licensing condition – that is, the logical form – downward-entailing (LF-DE) environment. An environment is LF-DE if and only if it permits a superset to be replaced by a subset on the level of LF. The LF-DE licensing condition thus states that polarity items in Mandarin Chinese can only be licensed in these LF-DE environments. Under this new licensing condition, monotonicity is no longer a relevant factor for comparing two sentences containing a superset and a subset, since LF-DE is not evaluated on the surface level, but rather on the logical level, as its name suggests.

Using the LF-DE condition, I will present a unified analysis of Mandarin Chinese NPIs and FCIs. At the same time, I will show that these two types of elements differ fundamentally in at least two respects. First, NPIs and FCIs differ from each in the quantificational power of the operator which binds them. Second, they differ in how they realize the domain-widening effect of the NP they follow; this effect may be realized along the quantity dimension or the quality dimension. However, since the main focus of my book is the licensing conditions of Chinese polarity items, I will not delve deeply into this issue of the distinction between FCIs and NPIs. Indeed, most previous studies on Chinese polarity items ignore this distinction altogether, using either NPI or FCI as a blanket term to refer to both types of elements.

1.4 Studies on Chinese polarity items

1.4.1 *The non-interrogative use of* wh-*indefinites in Chinese*

The ability for *wh*-elements in Chinese (and Japanese and Korean) to host a non-interrogative interpretation has already been discussed extensively in the literature; these are the so-called '*wh*-indeterminates' written about by Kuroda (1965). Ding et al. (1961) distinguished two basic uses of *wh*-indefinites, which they labeled *renzhi* (roughly equivalent to 'universal quantificational force') and *xuzhi* (roughly equivalent to 'existential quantificational force'). Since that early work, other scholars, including Yu (1965) and Lü (1985), have expanded on our understanding of these two types of Chinese indefinites. More recently, Shao (1996) presented a large number of examples of *wh*-indefinites and specified eight kinds of environments in which the non-interrogative *shenme* can appear. Some researchers have defined and described the various uses of Chinese *wh*-words based on their interaction with polarity sensitivity (Huang, 1982; Cheng, 1991; Li, 1992; Lin, 1998; Liao, 2011, among others); I will discuss some of this work in the next section.

1.4.1.1 Cheng (1991) and Li (1992)

Cheng (1991) proposed that *wh*-words in Mandarin Chinese are much like indefinite NPs, in the sense that they can be interpreted as non-quantificational variables whose semantic values depend on some element that binds them in the sentence (cf. Heim, 1982). Thus, on Cheng's account, the binder of a *wh*-word is key to its interpretation. Example (44) provides some illustrations of the effect of different binders. In (44a), the *wh*-word *shei* is bound by the question particle *ne* (which can also be covert, expressed by prosodic means), and receives a standard interrogative reading. However, in (44b), the *wh*-word *shenme* is bound by the universal quantifier *dou* 'all', and instead receives a universal reading. Finally, in (44c), *shenme* is licensed by negation (*bu*) and receives an existential reading.

(44) a   Ta gen shei shuohua ne?   (Interrogative)
        he TO who talk NE
        'Who is he talking to?'
    b   *Shenme*ta *dou* yao.   (Universal)
        what he all ask for
        'He asked for everything.'
    c   Ta *bu* xihuan shenme.   (Existential)
        he not like what
        'He doesn't like anything.'

Cheng suggests that 'environments in which this reading arises fall within the standard negative polarity environments' (Cheng, 1991).

A similar view is expressed in Li (1992), who further observes that, in addition to the standard polarity environments, existential *wh*-indefinites can also occur in complements of non-factive verbs such as *yiwei* 'think', in tentative statements with words like *dagai/ke'neng* 'probably', and in circumstantial *le* contexts where the truth value is not asserted directly. Li points out that the environments that license existential *wh*-indefinites in Mandarin Chinese share the property of having a truth value that is not directly fixed. To capture this observation, she proposes a non-positively-fixed truth condition for existential *wh*-indefinites. Li's explanation of the contexts in which existential *wh*-indefinites occur can be summarized as follows:

(45) a   contexts where the truth value is negated: negation;
   b   contexts where the truth value is not fixed: questions, conditionals, non-factive verb complements;
   c   contexts where the truth value is not asserted directly: seem, probably context, circumstantial *le*.

The semantic requirements of a non-positively-fixed truth condition, however, is not sufficient to explain why existential indefinites do not occur in the subject position of negative sentences or A-not-A questions. To account for this gap, Li proposes that existential indefinites and their licensors are subject to a structural requirement, which states that the licensor must c-command the existential indefinite at S-structure. This requirement rules out examples like the following (all examples in (46) are from Li, 1992).

(46) a   * shenme ren bu xihuan ta.
         what man not like he
         'Someone/anyone does not like him.'
   b   * Ta bu lai dui *shenme ren* zui hao.
         he not come to what man most good
         'That he does not come is the best for someone.'
   c   * Ta bu-gaoxing de zuo shenme.
         he not-happy DE do what
         'He did something unhappily.'
   d   * *shenme ren* xi-bu-xihuan ta
         what man like-not-like him
         'Does someone like him?'
   e   * Ruguo wo xihuan ta, *shenme ren* hui hen gaoxing
         if I like him what man will very happy
         'If I like him, somebody will be very happy.'

All of the examples in (46) are ungrammatical because of a failure of c-command. In (46a), for instance, the negative marker occurs lower than the subject *wh*-indefinite in syntactic tree structure. As a result, the former does not c-command the latter, and the sentence is ungrammatical. In (b), the negative marker is in an embedded clause and thus, again, does not c-command the *wh*-indefinite in the matrix clause. In (c), the negative morpheme is part of a lexical entry – i.e., it is a prefix – and so does not c-command the *wh*-indefinite, while in (d), the A-not-A operator does not c-command the subject *wh*-indefinite either. (As a side note: it is this example of the A-not-A operator that motivated Li to propose that the structural requirement is met at S-structure rather than at LF. The reason for this is that Li adopts Huang's

(1982) assumption that A-not-A operators move to Comp at LF. Under this assumption, a structural requirement of c-command at LF would incorrectly predict (46d) to be well-formed.) Finally, in (e), *ruguo* 'if' in the antecedent clause does not c-command the *wh*-indefinite in the consequent clause. Therefore, (a) through (e) are all ruled out by the structural c-command requirement. However, this is not the only possible explanation; later in this book, I will show that all these ungrammatical sentences can also be accounted for by a downward-entailing requirement at LF, which I will argue is the true licensing environment of Chinese polarity items.

In Chapter 6 of this study, I will account for the syntactic relation between *wh*-indefinites and their licensing operators by appealing to Hamblin semantics. In Hamblin semantics, indeterminate pronouns introduce alternatives that keep expanding until they find an operator to select them. Once this semantic concept is incorporated into the analysis of *wh*-indefinite licensing, the c-commanding relationship connecting *wh*-polarity items and their licensing operators is no longer relevant, whether defined at surface or deep structure.

1.4.1.2 Lin (1998)

Building on the work of Li (1992) and Lin (1998) shows that non-interrogative existential *wh*-phrases – typically referred to as existential polarity *wh*-phrases (EPWs) in Chinese – behave like polarity items. More specifically, Lin shows that such polarity *wh*-phrases appear in three kinds of environments, as follows:

(47) Group A: negation, questions and *if*-clauses
Group B: epistemic modality environments
Group C: some types of 'future' environments

Having defined these environments, he then generalizes the distribution of EPWs by appealing to the non-entailment-of-existence condition (NEEC), as shown below.

(48) Non-entailment-of-existence condition on EPWs (NEEC)
The use of an EPW is felicitous iff the local proposition in which the EPW appears does not entail existence of a referent satisfying the description of the EPW.

The range of environments that sanction EPWs is quite wide, including negation, questions, *if*-clauses, modal environments, some verb complements, some consequent clauses, imperatives and others. However, according to Lin (1998), this entire range of environments can be broadly classified into three groups, based on their decreasing strength for licensing polarity licensing. As the strength of each type of environment decreases, Lin observes an increasing need for the EPW to be accompanied by a classifier such as *ge* or *dian*. For example, consider

20 *Polarity theories and polarity phenomena*

the following three sentences, which Lin argues belong to the three groups of environments, respectively.

(49) Wo mei mai (*ge) shenme (dongxi) (Group A)
 I not buy *Cl what thing
 'I didn't buy anything.'
(50) Kongpa ta you shenme hua yao shuo (Group B)
 afraid he have what word want say
 'I am afraid that he has something to say.'
(51) Wo mingtian hui qu mai *(ge) shenme dongxi song ta de (Group C)
 I tomorrow will go buy *Cl what thing give him Par
 'I will go to buy something for him.'

Notice that if the classifier *ge* in (51) is deleted, the sentence becomes less grammatical, or even ungrammatical. Lin presents this linguistic fact, but leaves the explanation open.

Wu (2000) builds on Lin's work and this unanswered question, trying to explain why the non-interrogative readings of Chinese *wh*-phrases must be accompanied by a classifier in some contexts. To capture this fact, he suggests that the classifier must have, in some sense, the properties of a licensor of EWPs. Wu (2000) further argues that these Chinese classifiers have dual functions: they sometimes behave as a functional category, which can license some indefinite NPs/*wh*-NPs, and sometimes as a lexical category. On Wu's analysis, the negative polarity *wh*-items have a feature bundle containing several pairs of features, including [+interrogative/-interrogative] and [definite/indefinite]. When a classifier occurs with a *wh*-phrase, its features merge with the features of the *wh*-items, causing the existential interpretation to surface and suppressing the interrogative reading.

A major argument against Wu's analysis is the fact that sentence (45) is not acceptable if *shenme* and *ge* co-occur. If the [+indefinite] feature of *shenme* enters into an agreement relationship with the feature of the classifier *ge* as Wu postulates, no such incompatibility should occur. In this book, I will argue that the classifiers *ge*, *dianr* and the like play a different sort of role: they add attributive elements to the NPIs that follow them. The licensing function of these classifiers comes from these covert attributives they bear, which induce a tripartite structure and a downward-entailing context for polarity items. Section 4.5.3 of this study deals in detail with the question of why some polarity items require *ge* or *dianr* in some contexts. In that section, I will also present another strong argument for the downward-entailing approach and against the non-veridicality approach.

As I mentioned earlier, research into Chinese *wh*-indefinites has typically failed to distinguish FCIs from NPIs. In particular, most research in this area has tended to argue that the two types of polarity items have the same licensing conditions. Since, one the one hand, we do not have particularly convincing evidence to divide the same form into two functions, and at the same time, we have seen that existential *wh*-indefinites and universal *wh*-indefinites have more similarities than differences, in this work, I will follow previous research and treat the two as a unified type.

1.4.2 *Renhe*

The two distinctive uses of *any* in English have received a lot of attention in the literature, as we have seen above; see Horn (2000) for a comprehensive review of these discussions. It is well-known that *renhe* in Mandarin Chinese shares the two distinctive semantic properties of English *any* – that is, it can have both NPI and FCI readings. The comparison of *renhe* and *any* is illustrated in the following example. Examples (52)–(56) illustrate comparative examples of a negative sentence, modal sentence, question, conditional, and generic sentence, respectively.

(52) a   * Ta zuotian jiandao le renhe xuesheng
          he yesterday see LE *any* student
          * 'He met *any* student yesterday.'
    b   Ta zuotian mei jiandao *renhe* xuesheng
          he yesterday not see *any* student
          'He did not meet *any* student yesterday.'
(53) Ni bixu zhuazhu ta gei ni de renhe jihui
      you must grasp he give you DE any chance
      'You must grasp any chance that he gives you.'
(54) Ni zuotian gei ta mai le renhe dongxi ma?
      you yesterday give he buy LE any thing PAT
      'Did you buy him anything yesterday?'
(55) Ni yaoshi yudao renhe wenti, jiu qu zhao laoshi
      You if meet any problem JIU go look for teacher
      'If you meet with any problem, go and see the teacher.'
(56) Renhe maotouying dou zhua laoshu
      any owl all hunt mouse
      'Any owl hunts mice.'

As these Chinese sentences and their corresponding English translations show, Chinese *renhe* and English *any* behave almost identically semantically and syntactically. Morphologically, however, the two are quite different from each other. English *any* clearly consists of only one morpheme, and there is nothing indicating that it bears any additional meanings beyond negative polarity or free choice. *Renhe*, on the other hand, consists of two morphemes: a prefix *ren-*and a suffix-*he*. The prefix *ren means* 'regardless/as you please' and the suffix *he* means 'which' (in Classical Chinese). This morphology of *renhe* makes it comparable to some FCIs in certain other languages, including Greek, Spanish and Dutch, which also contain a morpheme meaning 'regardless' (or bearing an emphasizing function) and a *wh*-part (cf. Giannakidou, 2001; Haspelmath, 1997). For example, Table 1.2 shows the respective morphology of the Greek FCIs *anyone, anything, anywhere* and *anytime*:

(57)

Table 1.2

FCIs	Prefix	Infix	Suffix
Anyone	o-	pjos-	Dhipote
Anything	o-	yi-	Dhipote
Anywhere	o-	pu-	Dhipote
Anytime	o-	pote-	Dhipote

The Greek FCIs *opjosdhipote, otidhipote, opudhipote* and *opotedhipote* share the same mechanism of morphology as we observed with the element *renhe* in Mandarin Chinese. In the Greek case, the particle contains three segments: *o-* 'the' (prefix); *-pjos-* 'who', *-ti-* 'what', *-pu-* 'where1' or *-pote-* 'where2' (infix) and an additional emphasizing element *-dhipote* (suffix).

Despite their apparent interpretive similarity, however, the licensing environments of English *any* and Chinese *renhe* are not identical. Compare the following Chinese sentences with *renhe*, which are licit, with their putative counterparts with *any* in English, which are not. As the examples illustrate, these sentences use the universal quantifier *every* in English instead.

(58) a   Ta qu guo zhege chengshi de renhe yi ge jiaoluo
       he go GUO this city DE *any* one CL corner
       'He has been to *any/every corner of this city.'
    b * Ta qu **le** zhege chengshi de *renhe* yi ge jiaoluo
       he go LE this city DE *any* one CL corner
       Intended: 'He has been to every corner of this city.'
    c Zhege shijieshang cunzai zhe *renhe* buke'neng de shiqing
       this world exist ZHE *any* impossible DE thing
       'There exists *anything/everything impossible in the world.'

While the sentences in (58) illustrate the contrasting distribution of *any* and *renhe*, the contrast between (58a) and (58b) also displays the different behaviors of *renhe* when it occurs with the experiential marker *guo* and the perfective marker *le*. *Le* marks a typical positive episodic sentence in Chinese, while *guo* presents a class of events rather than a single one. One possible explanation as to why *guo* is compatible with *renhe* but *le* is not is that *guo* has more modal characteristics. I will pursue the question of how modality relates to polarity items in the later part of this book.

Renhe differs from the Mandarin Chinese *wh*-indefinites like *shenme* in its morphological structure. In Chapter 6 of this study, I will investigate the different morphological structures of *renhe* and *shenme* (as the representative *wh*-indefinite), and propose that *renhe*, as a universal quantifier, functions as a FCI, whereas *shenme* is a NPI and frequently functions as an existential quantifier. I will explore the non-uniformity of Chinese polarity items in more detail at that time.

1.4.3 Strong/weak NPIs and Kuo (2003)

Zwarts (1998) proposed three laws of negative polarity, as follows:

(59) Zwarts' laws of negative polarity:

    a   Only sentences in which an expression of sub-minimal negation occurs can contain a negative polarity item of the weak type.

    b   Only sentences in which an expression of minimal negation occurs can contain a negative polarity item of the strong type.

    c   Only sentences in which an expression of classical negation occurs can contain a negative polarity item of the super-strong type.

To support these laws, Zwarts proposed a hierarchy of sub-minimal, minimal and classical negation, shown in (60), arguing that this hierarchy is a linguistic reflection of the underlying hierarchy of monotone-decreasing, anti-additive, and anti-morphic functions as shown in Table 1.3.

(60)

Table 1.3

Name	Logical properties	
Expression of sub-minimal negation	1	$f(x \cup y) \subseteq f(x) \cap f(y)$
	2	$f(x) \cup f(y) \subseteq f(x \cap y)$
Expression of minimal negation	1	$f(x \cup y) = f(x) \cap f(y)$
	2	$f(x) \cup f(y) \subseteq (x \cap y)$
Expression of classical negation	1	$f(x \cup y) = f(x) \cap f(y)$
	2	$f(x) \cap f(y) \subseteq f(x \cap y)$
	3	$f(-x) = -f(x)$

Zwarts (1993) brings together a series of earlier observations by various authors to show that not all NPIs are equal. Specifically, Zwarts defines three classes of NPIs, which he calls 'weak', 'strong' and 'super-strong', and gives them each an algebraic characterization, describing the contexts that can host these different types of NPIs. Weak NPIs, like *any* or *ever*, are presumably unstressed and require downward-entailing contexts. Strong NPIs, like *any student at all*, or *lift a finger* need an anti-additive context (iff f(X∪Y) = f(X)∩f(Y)). Finally, superstrong NPIs like *one bit* require an 'anti-morphic' context (iff f(–X) = –f(X)).

Krifka (1995) identifies a problem for Zwarts (1993); he notes that there seems to be an interesting relationship between NPI types and stress, which Zwarts did not mention and which does not follow straightforwardly from his analysis. Krifka's observation is this: although, as a general rule, weak NPIs are unstressed, whereas strong NPIs attract stress, strong NPIs do not always carry the main stress of a sentence. In particular, contrastive stress overrides stress on strong NPIs (as in *JOHN didn't lift a finger to help me, not MARY*).

In making this observation, Krifka (1995) poses the following question: Why is it that certain types of polarity items only occur in certain contexts? He proposes that this is due to a peculiar interaction between the meaning of polarity items and the expressions in which they occur, together with certain general pragmatic rules that come along with the illocutionary force of the sentence.

As for the distribution of weak and strong NPIs, Krifka accounts for this by arguing that weak NPIs do not occur in emphatic assertions, and that strong NPIs do not occur in regular (scalar) assertions. Weak NPIs are in fact ruled out for emphatic assertions because their meaning is not 'extreme' enough for a felicitous emphatic assertion. Strong NPIs, on the other hand, are non-exhaustive, and therefore fine with emphatic NPIs.

This foundational work on strong and weak NPIs is imported to Mandarin Chinese by Kuo (2003), who argues that NPIs in Chinese are non-homogeneous, and the classes of licensors for these four types of negative polarity items correspond to the hierarchy of negativity in the sense of Zwarts (1998) and Giannakidou (1998): non-veridical operators, downward-entailing operators, anti-additive operators, and anti-morphic operators.

The degree of negativity matches the following hierarchy: non-veridical operator>downward-entailing operator>anti-additive operator>anti-morphic operator. Based on this hierarchy, Kuo unifies the account of Mandarin Chinese NPIs as follows: indefinite *wh*-phrases are licensed by non-veridical operators; NPI *any* is licensed by downward-entailing operators; NPI *renhe* is licensed by anti-additive operators; NPI-minimizers are licensed by anti-morphic operators.

It is a convenient outcome of Kuo's theory that the four types of operators happen to correspond to the four classes of NPI licensors. However, despite its symmetrical appearance, I will contend in this book that Kuo's analysis of Chinese NPIs is inaccurate from both a theoretical and empirical perspective. Counterexamples against Kuo's analysis are numerous. Recall, for example, that Kuo argues that indefinite *wh*-phrases are licensed by non-veridical operators in Mandarin. However, it is very easy to find grammatical sentences with *wh*-polarity items in them; one need merely look at *dou* sentences:

(60) shenme ren dou canjia le toupiao
 what person all attend le vote
 'All the people voted.'

(61) shei dou jujue le ta de yaoqing
 who all refuse le his invitation
 'People all refused his invitation.'
(62) Na-ge xuesheng dou jige le
 Which-CL student all pass le
 'All students have passed.'

All these three sentences would be ungrammatical on Kuo's analysis, since they are all veridical sentences. The aspectual marker *le* marks the episodic property of each sentence in question. Since it is impossible to say all sentences with *dou* are non-veridical, it is inaccurate to say *wh*-indeterminates can only be licensed by non-veridical operators; they can clearly appear in *dou* sentences quite freely.

Beyond these empirical concerns, Kuo's hypobook also faces a serious methodological problem. In Kuo (2003), *shenme, renhe, any* and Chinese minimizers are all talked about. In Kuo (2003), the author tries to capture a number of different polarity items from different languages – including *shenme, renhe*, English *any* and Chinese minimizers – under the same standard with respect to the hierarchy of negation. It is odd to conduct a comparison of several Chinese polarity items and one English polarity item all on the same level. Furthermore, it is difficult to explain under such an analysis why an *any*-like element is missing in Mandarin Chinese and the Mandarin polarity items instead constitute a discontinuous hierarchy.

Kuo's (2003) analysis of Mandarin Chinese NPIs adopts Giannakidou and Cheng's idea that polarity items in Mandarin are sensitive to (non)veridicality. As previewed in this chapter, in this book I will argue that (non)veridicality is not the determinant of Chinese polarity items. I dismiss Kuo's assessment on the basis of its empirical and theoretical inadequacy, and present counterexamples to Kuo's claims by demonstrating that all kinds of NPIs can readily appear to the left of *dou*. These phenomena have been taken as only appearing in Chinese polarity phenomena according to previous studies such as Yuan (2007), Cheng and Giannakidou (2005, 2013) and Jiang (2015). I believe this is the wrong analytical path. Instead, in this study, I will depart from these previous authors in analyzing sentences with *dou* as part of a tripartite structure containing a universal quantificational operator. I will treat *dou*'s licensing of NPIs as one of the ways Mandarin Chinese realizes the downward-entailing condition, or more precisely, the LF-DE condition. However, just because NPIs have to obey the LF-DE licensing condition, this is not to say they are all the same.

This chapter sets the stage for the rest of the book by introducing the topics covered in Chapters 2–7. Chapter 2 introduces the non-veridicality approach to polarity items, and then investigates a range of evidence indicating that this approach is insufficient to explain Chinese polarity sensitivity. The properties of the pre-*dou* position are shown to be particularly problematic for the non-veridicality approach. In Chapter 3, I apply the tripartite structural framework to the analysis of *dou* in Mandarin by tracing the work of several previous investigations. Chapter 4 considers the role that *dou* plays in licensing Mandarin polarity items. I explore in detail the quantificational properties of *dou*, including its tripartite structure, its universal quantificational power, and the cardinality requirement of its first argument. All these properties play a role in determining how *dou* functions to license polarity items. Chapter 5 builds on this basic understanding of *dou* by examining its properties and behavior with respect to modality. This investigation also helps shed light on *dou*'s licensing of polarity items. The licensing condition for Chinese polarity items is updated to state that non-interrogative *wh*-indeterminates in Mandarin can be licensed in the restriction domain of a necessity operator, following Heim's analysis of modality. Chapter 6 considers the non-uniformity of Chinese polarity items. Chapter 7 concludes the book.

2 Non-veridicality approach and the challenge from *dou* sentences

2.1 Problems for Cheng and Giannakidou (2005, 2013)

As I mentioned in the last chapter, setting aside traditional descriptions, all modern linguistic research on Chinese polarity items follows an approach consistent with the analyses of Giannakidou and Zwarts. Specifically, these studies all take non-veridicality to be the licensor of Chinese polarity items. Two foundational studies that attempted to capture this generalization were Lin (1998), who proposed the non-entailment-of-existence condition, and Li (1992), who proposed the non-positively-fixed truth condition. The generalizations developed by Lin and Li were reformulated by Cheng and Giannakidou (2005, 2013) in terms of non-veridicality and intensionality.

Giannakidou (2001) proposed that free-choice items (FCIs) are intensional, in the sense that they contain a dependent-world variable that cannot be free, but must be bound by some operator. Two types of operators are possible: either a Q-operator, or a λ-operator. Cheng and Giannakidou (2005) adopt this claim and apply it to Mandarin Chinese, arguing that Chinese FCIs are indeed indefinites that contain such variables. On their analysis, the free-choice determiner is treated as a property modifier which, when applied to the NP denotation, returns an intensionalized property as its output:

(1) $[[\text{DETFC}]] = \lambda P_{<e, t>}. \lambda x \lambda w[P(x)(w)]$

This expression says that the free-choice determiner takes a property P (that is, a set of individuals x that have the property P) as input, and returns a function from individuals x to worlds w such that x belongs to the extension of the predicate P in w. This operation is known as intensionalizing the NP argument. Intensionalization can be understood as the creation of an open w variable position – and it is this function that forms the core of free choice.

Building on this theoretical framework, Cheng and Giannakidou (2005, 2013) propose that free-choice *wh*-indeterminates need not be uniform – and in fact are not, at least in Mandarin Chinese. The authors distinguish three types of FCIs in Mandarin Chinese, illustrated by the following three sentences.

(2) a Women neng-gou zhan-sheng renhe kun-nan
       we can fight-win *any* difficulty
       'We can conquer *any* difficulty.'
    b *Na*-zhong hua-se *dou* xing.
       which-kind flower-color all possible
       '*Any* kind of flower-color is possible.'
    c Zhe-ge haizi *shenme dou* bu pa.
       this-CL child what all not afraid
       'This child is not afraid of anything.'

As these sentences illustrate, Mandarin Chinese can express free choice with *wh*-indefinites in three different ways: through the *wh*-word *renhe* (from Classical Chinese *ren* 'regardless/as you please', plus *he* 'which') combined with a NP (2a); through the *wh*-word *na*-('which') combined with a classifier and an NP (2b); or through one of a number of bare *wh*-words, including *shei* 'who', *shenme* 'what' and *nar* 'where' (2c).

Cheng and Giannakidou argue that these three types of Chinese FCIs can be grouped into two varieties: intensional indeterminates (*na*-CL NP and *renhe* NP), and non-intensional ones (bare *wh*-indefinites). According to their proposal, the crucial difference between the two varieties is that the intensional indeterminates exhibit polarity behavior and are not licensed in veridical and episodic contexts, whereas the non-intensional indeterminates do not exhibit polarity behavior and can occur in episodic positive sentences. Some relevant examples are the following.

(3) a *Na-ge xuesheng dou jin-lai-le
       which-CL student all enter-come-PERF
       Intended: 'Anybody/everybody came in.'
    b *Renhe ren dou* jin-lai-le.
       any person all enter-come-PERF
       Intended: 'Anyone came in.'
(4) Shei dou jin-lai-le
    who all enter-come-PERF
    'Everyone came in.'

The fact that *le* in these examples is compatible with bare *wh*-indefinites (4) but incompatible with *renhe* + NP and *na*-CL + NP constructions (3) provides a useful test environment for determining which Mandarin Chinese FCIs can appear in episodic positive sentences. On Cheng and Giannakidou's analysis, this differential distribution of the two FCI varieties derives from their different behavior in terms of intensionalization (Giannakidou, 2001; Cheng and Giannakidou, 2005). Specifically, they argue that it is the presence of a dependent world variable that renders a *wh*-phrase polarity sensitive and restricts its distribution in non-episodic contexts; on their account, *na*-CL N + P and *renhe* + NP constructions contain such a variable.

If this analysis is on the right track, the next question is: which element induces the intensionalization for each type of FCI? For the *renhe* + NP construction, Cheng and Giannakidou pursue an etymological argument, arguing that *renhe* can be deconstructed into *ren* 'regardless' and *he* 'which' (Classical Chinese). Based on this lexical deconstruction, the authors argue that the free-choice determiner (*ren*) contained within the FCI provides its intensionality. For the *na*-CL + NP construction, Cheng and Giannakidou adopt Lin's (1996) suggestion that all *dou* sentences are underlyingly *wulun* 'regardless' . . . *dou* sentences (with the *wulun* element elided). Based on this assumption, Cheng and Giannakidou argue that the presence of (covert) *wulun* intensionalizes the FCI, creating the observed polarity behavior.

Although I disagree with Cheng and Giannakidou's non-veridicality approach to Mandarin Chinese polarity items, I agree with their assessment of how *dou* sentences are derived and how *renhe* and other *wh*-polarity items are differentiated morphologically. I will develop an argument based on their research in Chapter 6.

Cheng and Giannakidou use the same set of observations and arguments to explain the similarity between *renhe* + NPs and *na*-CL + NP constructions – i.e., the fact that neither type of FCI can appear in pure episodic perfective past contexts, as illustrated in (3a) and (3b). The authors argue that both of these sentences are inherently intensionalized, because they contain *ren* and *wulun*, respectively. Bare *wh*-indefinites, on the other hand, do not have a restricted dependent world variable, and can thus be independently bound, yielding a wider distribution – e.g., in episodic contexts like (4). In other words, bare *wh*-indefinites are ambiguous in that the world variable they contain may be dependent or independent. In free-choice contexts, the world variable is dependent, and in non-free-choice contexts, the world variable may be independent, bound by the actual world. This distinction not only explains the contrast between the two types of bare *wh*-indefinites, but also the contrast between bare *wh*-indefinites and *na*-CL + NP constructions.

Problematically, however, certain language facts that are fundamental for Cheng and Giannakidou's approach are not supported by native speaker judgments. Indeed, in some cases the data seem not just questionable, but entirely unacceptable. According to an informal survey I conducted with about 20 native speakers, the judgment Cheng and Giannakidou provide for (3) is not right: there is no contrast between bare *wh* constructions and *na*-CL + NPs with respect to veridicality. Further support for this conclusion comes from the corpus of the Chinese Linguistics Research Center of Peking University; I searched this corpus for instances of *shenme* + NP and found a number of episodic sentences with *na*-CL + NP and *renhe* + NP.

Besides this significant empirical problem, Cheng and Giannakidou's analysis also leaves open some important theoretical questions. For instance, their analysis provides no clear way to account for the very restricted distribution of the definite *na*-CL in modal contexts and its contrast with the other intensional FCI *renhe* in this respect. As the sentences in (5) show, although *renhe* can appear under the modal *keyi* 'can' in object position, bare *wh*-phrases and *na*-CL phrases cannot. When these latter two constructions appear in this context, they can take only the interrogative reading, but not a free-choice reading.

(5) a   Ta keyi jie renhe shu.
       he can borrow *any* book
       'He can borrow *any* book.'

b   *Ta keyi jie naben/*shenme* shu.
    he can borrow which/what book
    Not intended: 'He can borrow *any* book.'
    Intended: 'What book/which book can he borrow?'

Cheng and Giannakidou attempt to explain this contrast by appealing to the definiteness of *na*-CL. However, for them, definiteness in *na*-CL is neither a necessary nor a sufficient condition for a freer distribution of this class of FCIs.

Cheng and Giannakidou also appeal to definiteness to explain why constructions with *dou* can occur in an episodic environment. Specifically, they argue that *dou* turns an indefinite FCI into a definite one through functional licensing. Jiang (2015), however, criticizes this analysis, providing two arguments against Cheng and Giannakidou's assessment that *dou*'s definiteness licenses polarity items. First, Jiang contends that, in cases where the position to the left of *dou* is definite, the interpretation of definiteness arises from the whole sentence, including aspectual markers – not from *dou* itself. Second, Jiang points out that there are many sentences with *dou* that are generic or habitual. The subject position of these sentences is not definite at all. I consider Jiang's (2015) arguments to convincingly support his standpoint.

As for the classification of polarity items in Mandarin Chinese, I also disagree with Cheng and Giannakidou on this point: I do not believe that *na*-CL and *renhe* are intensionalized, whereas bare *shenme* is not. In what follows, I will propose that polarity items in Chinese can be classified into two groups, based on whether or not they contain a concessive element *ren* on the surface morphological level. On my analysis, *renhe* belongs to the group that does contain such a concessive element, while *shenme* and *na*-CL belong to the group that does not contain any concessive element. Thus, as I will argue extensively in this book, it is the *distributions* of these FCIs that determine their classification, not how they are derived from a morphological perspective.

Based on the above considerations, I believe that non-veridicality is neither a necessary nor a sufficient condition of polarity item licensing. To take just one example, consider epistemic possibility. Epistemic possibility arises through a non-veridical operator that typically (although not always) introduces an NPI-unfriendly environment:

(6) #It's likely that anyone will win.
(7) *na-ge ren haoxiang xihuan ta
    Which CL man likely like him
    Intended: 'It seems that everyone likes him.'

Both English *likely* and its Chinese counterpart *haoxiang* express a context of epistemic possibility, and neither is compatible with an NPI – *anyone* or *na-ge ren*, respectively. In the next section, I will dig deeper into the Mandarin Chinese data to highlight several places where problems arise for the non-veridicality approach to NPIs. At the same time, I will begin to illustrate the advantages of the downward-entailing approach.

2.2 Investigations

First, let's take a closer look at the distribution of polarity items, focusing first on polarity items in the form *na*-CL + NP. See the relevant data in Table 2.1.

(8)

Table 2.1

Affirmative episodic sentences	
1a *Wo mai le *na*-ben shu. I buy le which-CL book Intended: I bought some book.	1b. Wo *na*-ben shu *dou* mai le. I which-CL book dou buy le I bought every book.
2a *Wo mei mai *na*-ben shu. I not buy which-CL book Intended: I didn't buy *any* book.	2b Wo *na*-ben shu *dou* mei mai. I which-CL book *dou* not buy I didn't buy *any* book.

Notice that all four of the sentences in Table 2.1 are marked by declarative punctuation, strongly suggesting that they are to be interpreted (and their grammaticality, or ungrammaticality, assessed) as polarity constructions rather than interrogative constructions. The sentences labeled 1) and 2), a) and b) represent two dimensions of comparison, from different perspectives: 1) and 2) differ in negativity (1 is affirmative and 2 negative), while a) and b) differ in the presence of *dou* (and whether *na*-CL is placed in a pre-*dou* position). From the judgments shown in this table (8), we can conclude, minimally, that negation alone is not a sufficient condition for the licensing of *na*-CL as a polarity item; furthermore, we can conclude that polarity *na*-CL + NP constructions are not necessarily licensed by negation.

The grammatical episodic sentence in (8) (1b) is a direct counterexample to one of the tenets of Cheng and Giannakidou's (2005, 2013) analysis. Recall that these authors argued that *na*-CL is excluded from episodic sentences because it is intensionalized, but we have seen in the previous section and in Table 2.1 that the data do not support this analysis: the licensing condition of *na*-CL cannot be either non-episodicity or intensionality. Table 2.2 provides more data concerning this issue.

(9)

Table 2.2

Modal sentences	
1a*ni (*dou*) keyi jie *na*-ben shu you *dou* can borrow which-CL book Intended: You can borrow every book.	1bni *na*-ben shu *dou* keyi jie you which-CL book *dou* can borrow You can borrow every book.
2a*ni (*dou*) yinggai du *na*-ben shu you *dou* should read which-CL book Intended: You should read every book.	2bni *na*-ben shu *dou* yinggai du you which-CL book *dou* should read You should read every book.

32 Non-veridicality approach

As in (9), we can see that the *na*-CL constructions in these four sentences are all non-interrogative. The contrast between the a) and b) sentences also continues to remain the same as in Table 2.1; however, the contrast in 1) and 2) is different in this table. Now, the sentences in 1) and 2) differ in that they contain different sorts of modals. That is, 1) contains epistemic modals, such as *keyi* 'can', whereas 2) contains deontic modals, such as *yinggai* 'should'. Thus, we can conclude that polarity *na*-CL cannot be licensed by modal words. This is another piece of counter-evidence against Cheng and Giannakidou's analysis, since modal sentences are another type of intensional context.

Instead, in both tables, we can see that what is really vital to non-interrogative *na*-CLs is the appearance of *dou*. Furthermore, these *na*-CLs polarity items must be located before *dou* in the sentence. That is, they are always assigned to the restriction domain when the tripartite structure is mapped. Let's next check whether the same generalization holds in other licensing environments, such as questions and generic sentences as shown in Tables 2.3 and 2.4, respectively.

(10)

Table 2.3

Questions	
a *ni jie le *na*-ben shu ma? You borrow le which-CL book ma Intended: Did you borrow *any* book?	b ni *na*-ben shu *dou* jie le ma? You which-CL book *dou* borrow le ma Did you borrow every book?

Questions, which are also intensional, cannot license polarity *na*-CL items by virtue of their interrogative nature. It is commonly known that *wh*-elements can be interpreted as interrogative, existential, or universal, depending on the quantificational operator that accompanies them; however, as soon as an interrogative structure is used, the *wh*-element itself must necessarily be interpreted as interrogative. In the examples in Table 2.3, the intended meaning of the *na*-CL construction is polarity, rather than interrogative, but this interpretation is blocked because *na*-CL appears in a question. The polarity usage of *na*-CL in question is also dependent on the appearance of *dou* and the succession order of *na*-CL and *dou*.

(11)

Table 2.4

Generic sentences	
a *na-zhi maotouying zhua laoshu Which-CL owl hunt mouse Intended: Every owl hunts mice.	b na-zhi maotouying *dou* zhua laoshu which-CL owl *dou* hunt mouse Every owl hunts mice.

Generic sentences are intensional, in the sense that they are not anchored in one real world, but in a number of possible worlds. If the proposal about *dou* by Cheng and Giannakidou (2005, 2013) is on the right track, generic sentences should provide an acceptable environment for *dou*. However, this prediction is not supported by the facts. Without the contribution of *dou*, the interrogative operator cannot license a *na*-CL polarity item. Furthermore, even in grammatical questions with polarity *na*-CL phrases, it is not the interrogative itself, but *dou* that sanction them.

I have been referring to the kinds of sentences illustrated in Table 2.4 as 'generic' because these types of sentences are usually used to express kind and generalization readings. However, they can also be used to express the universal reading, which is slightly different from the generic reading in that the former disallows exceptions whereas the latter allows them. I will return to a more detailed discussion of the difference between generic sentences and universal sentences later in this book, with a separate aim. For the moment, let's set this difference aside, as it does not affect my main purpose: identifying and specifying the real factor responsible for the licensing of *na*-CL polarity items. Suffice it to note, for now, that the restriction domains of generic and universal sentences involve the same direction of entailment.

So far in this subsection, I have shown that intensionality is not a necessary or sufficient licensing condition for *na*-CL noun phrases with non-interrogative meaning. Instead, I have suggested that a pre-*dou* position is sufficient for the licensing. Next, let's turn to some other environments, besides *dou* sentences, where polarity items can be licensed. Consider the following two sentences in Table 2.5.

(12)

Table 2.5

Conditionals

---

1. Ruguo *na*-ge *ren* **gan** beipan guojia, jiu hui zao *ren* tuoqi
   If which-CL person dare betray country then will encounter spurn
   If someone dares to betray his country, he will be spurned.
2. Ruguo *na*-ge *ren* beipan le guojia, jiu hui zao *ren* tuoqi
   If which-CL person betray le country then will encounter spurn
   If someone betrayed his country, he will be spurned.
3. Ruguo *na*-ge *ren dou* beipan le guojia, zhege guojia jiu bucunzai le
   If which-CL person *dou* betray le country, this country will not exist le
   If all the people betrayed the country, this country will not exist anymore.

As these sentences illustrate, here is another context in which *na*-CL noun phrases can be licensed. In the first and second sentences above, the *na*-CL construction appears licit in the antecedent clause of a *ruguo*-conditional, no matter whether the protasis itself is intensional or episodic. Clearly, the presence of *dou* is not necessary in these two cases for the licensing of the *na*-CL polarity items. On the other hand, *dou* clearly does contribute some other meaning to the sentence that is not active in the absence of *dou*. We can see this contrast when we compare the second and third sentences in (12). The protasis in 2) is uttered when it is not clear to the speaker whether there exists a person who betrays his country. By contrast, 3) can only be uttered in a situation where there has already been at least one person who betrayed his country. *Na*-CL noun phrases that contain *dou* thus express universal quantification and requires the extension of *na*-CL + NP to be non-empty. That is why sentence 3) is different from sentence 2) in its presupposition of the existence of a traitor.

Sentence 1) above is presented to show that *na*-CL polarity items in *ruguo . . . name . . .* sentences can be licensed by an antecedent clause without any help from other factors, like modals. In my analysis as follows, I will argue that the antecedent clause is mapped into the restriction domain of a universal quantification, where it meets the LF downward-entailing requirement for licensing polarity items.

Next, let's take a look at the behavior of *na*-CL polarity items in the context of negation for Table 2.6.

(13)

Table 2.6

Negation with the help of ye	
1a *wo mai le *na*-ben shu I buy le which-CL book Intended: I bought some book.	1b *wo *na*-ben shu *ye* mai le I which-CL book even buy le Intended: I bought some book.
2a *wo mei mai na-ben shu I not buy which-CL book Intended: I did not buy any book.	2b wo na-ben shu ye mei mai I which-CL book even not buy I did not buy any book.

The 1) and 2) sentences in this table show a positive versus negative interpretation, respectively, while the a) and b) sentences compare the presence versus absence of the element *ye*, roughly translated as *even* or *also*. We can see from these examples that *na*-CL polarity items are only licit if both conditions hold: (i) the polarity item falls within the scope of negation and (ii) the sentence contains *ye*. Among the four sentences above, the one that meets both these conditions is the only grammatical one.

Contrast this with the situation in diagram (9), where appearing ahead of *dou* in the sentence was sufficient licensing for the non-interrogative *na*-CL noun phrase to appear. The data in this table allow us to add a new entry to the roster of places where *na*-CL polarity items can appear: the pre-*ye* 'also' position of negation sentences is another valid context for these items.

Shenme noun phrases behave identically to *na*-CL noun phrases with respect to their distributions in affirmative episodic sentences, modals, questions, generic sentences, conditionals and negative sentences with *ye*. That is, if we replaced *na*-CL with *shenme* in sentences (8) to (13), the results would not change: the same sentences would still be grammatical, and the same ones ungrammatical. Similarly, the third polarity item *renhe* shows nearly all of the same distributional restrictions as *shenme* and *na*-CL. The one exception is observed when *renhe* appears in the object position of a modal sentence. Unlike *wh*-polarity items, *renhe* is licit in that position. This is a curious restriction from the point of view of Cheng and Giannakidou's non-veridicality hypothesis: modals are typical non-veridical contexts, yet of the three types of polarity items in Mandarin Chinese, modal sentences can only license *renhe* in the object position. When I turn to the particular distribution of *renhe* later in this work, I will show that the real licensing factor here is not the modal.

In the next section, I will argue that all these problems I have raised with the non-veridicality approach can be solved if the downward-entailing approach is adopted instead for the analysis of polarity items. To prepare for this analysis, I would first like to draw together the evidence from the earlier investigation to consider the true distribution of Chinese polarity items. It seems clear from the evidence presented that these items are not sensitive to the distinction between veridical and non-veridical contexts. Rather, they appear in the following three environments:

(14)　① The antecedent of conditionals
　　　② Negation (with *ye*)
　　　③ The restriction domain of a universal quantifier, such as *dou*

A following question arises naturally from this generalization: are the three licensing environments of non-interrogative *na*-CL independent of one another, or are they linked in some significant way? Does a common interpretive or structural feature underlie their apparently different surface configurations? I will argue that the essential property underlying all these environments – and thus, the real determining factor responsible for the licensing of non-interrogative *na*-CL noun phrases – is the downward-entailing property of the position the polarity items occupy.

2.3 The comparison between Liao (2011) and the present work

My analysis shares with the work of Liao (2011) an important insight about the non-veridicality approach to Chinese polarity items. Liao, too, notes that the pre-*dou* position is a very frequent host environment for Chinese polarity items, but that these *dou* sentences are not always non-veridical. In fact, most of them are affirmative utterances bearing the typical episodic marker *le*. See the following example:

(15)　Na-ge/shenme/renhe xuesheng dou tongguo le kaohe
　　　Which-CL/what/any student all pass le assessment
　　　'All students have passed the assessment.'

Despite beginning from this similar observation, however, Liao (2011) and I treat this problem in different ways. Liao sets about to defend the non-veridicality approach by adding more detailed principles. In contrast, I argue that we should move away from non-veridicality as a solution to Chinese polarity items, instead turning to an account based on the traditional downward-entailing approach. We have already seen that the non-veridicality approach has been refuted by Horn (2000) from a theoretical perspective – and the Mandarin Chinese data I provided in the previous sections constitute further evidence against it. The fundamental trouble with Liao's account is that the approach she defends and the remedy she offers are not compatible with each other. She used Chierchia's bi-dimension (2006) (alternative semantics) to analyze *dou* as a focus marker that introduces alternatives that perform domain widening. This domain widening results in a stronger statement under a negative (or, more generally, downward-entailing) context, in accordance with Gricean principles.

Yet the domain-widening theory that Liao embraces can only be applied if one first acknowledges the downward-entailing approach. Indeed, the notion of domain widening was originally raised to answer the question of why polarity items can be licensed in a downward-entailing environment (Kadmon and Landman, 1993). Without the help of a downward-entailing context, domain widening alone cannot provide an acceptable environment for Mandarin Chinese polarity items. Thus, Liao's reliance on the domain-widening theory is insufficient to save an approach that does not take downward entailment into account.

Liao also argues that *dou* turns the FCI into some kind of definite noun phrase in order to fit the environment. In this, she follows Cheng and Giannakidou, who also treat *dou* as a definiteness-maker. However, we have seen above that (i) a definite environment is not necessary for an FCI to occur, and (ii) definiteness does not come from the function of *dou*.

The advantage of my analysis is that I use one approach consistently to account for all the Chinese polarity phenomena: in all cases, the polarity item must be licensed in a downward-entailing environment. I stick to this approach throughout my analysis, making minor adjustments within the same frame. That is consistent with the purpose of this book: to investigate how to justify the constraints of the downward-entailing analysis, and to work out in detail how the semantics of the problematic constructions have to work in order for these moves to successfully rescue the downward-entailing approach. To foreshadow the approach I will take in the following chapters, I will introduce a tripartite structure as a linguistic tool to reanalyze *dou* sentences where polarity items appear, and argue that downward entailment at LF should replace surface downward entailing as the licensing condition. First, however, I turn to reconsider the status of *dou*.

2.4 Is *dou* a maximality operator?

Like other scholars who have studied *dou*, I agree that the readings of this particle can be unified, but not by appealing to its role as a maximality operator (also known as an iota operator), as Xiang (2008) and Cheng and Giannakidou (2005, 2013) have proposed. Instead, I return to the traditional, standard view of *dou* as a universal quantifier.

Let's recall the challenge that *dou* poses to the non-veridicality approach to Chinese polarity items: as we saw in previous sections, the pre-*dou* position is a very common environment for Chinese polarity items, but these *dou* sentences in which the polarity items occur are not always non-veridical. Thus, it is important that we dig deeper into the function of *dou* and its interaction with polarity items.

The element *dou* in Mandarin, which is typically glossed as 'all', has been a popular topic of Chinese linguistics (see Lee, 1996; Cheng, 1991; Jiang, 1998; Lin, 1998). As we saw above, Cheng and Giannakidou (2005, 2013), among others, have argued that *dou* encodes a maximality operator (iota operator), and that it is this operator that gives rise to the polarity licensing of *dou*. Xiang (2008) expands this analysis to incorporate different uses of *dou* – including distributivity and scalar interpretations as well as polarity licensing. However, this 'maximality operator' analysis diverges sharply from the traditional view on *dou*, which takes it to be a universal adverb or a distributive element.

Cheng and Giannakidou (2005, 2013) also consider the contribution of *dou* in licensing Chinese FCIs. They draw on their analysis of *dou* as a maximality (iota) operator, arguing that it takes an intensionalized property as its input and returns a maximal plural individual, as shown in (16):

(16) $[[dou]] = \lambda P/(\lambda x \,.P(x))$

Crucial to Cheng and Giannakidou's argument is the fact that *dou* by itself doesn't directly license FCIs. Rather, it operates on an intensionalized domain. For example, in an episodic context (17), the *wh*-FCI *na-ge xuesheng* 'which student' cannot be licensed by the presence of *dou* alone (at least, according to the authors' assessment. This generalization may be inaccurate, as we shall see below). In this case, it is the combination of *dou* and the modal context that meets the licensing condition, as shown in the grammatical version of the sentence in (18).

(17) *Na-ge xuesheng dou jinlai-le
Which-Cl student *dou* enter-Perf
'Every/*any* student entered.'
(18) Na-ge xuesheng dou keyi jinlai
Which-Cl student *dou* can enter.
'Every/*any* student can enter.'

However, the (un)grammaticality of sentence (17) is a matter of debate. According to a survey I conducted with ten native speakers of Mandarin Chinese, this sentence, with *dou* but no modal, is acceptable. This result also matches my native speaker intuition. Furthermore, as I noted above, a corpus-based data analysis shows that *dou* alone can license *na*-CL polarity items perfectly well. See the following illustrative examples:

(19) Zhe-ci qimo kaoshi suiran hen nan, dan na-ge xuesheng dou jige le
This time final exam though very hard which-Cl student dou pass le.
'Every student passed the final exam though it was really very hard for them this time.'
(20) Zai shangshiji kangri zhanzheng zhong, jihu na-ge zhongguoren dou canjia le zhandou.
In last century Anti-Japanese War almost which-CL Chinese dou participant le battle
'Almost all the Chinese people participated in the Anti-Japanese War of the last century.'

Based on this evidence, Cheng and Giannakidou's generalization – that *na*-CLs cannot appear in episodic sentences and are sensitive to intensionalized contexts – appears to be incorrect. Instead, it appears that what is really crucial for the licensing for *na*-CLs like *na-ge xuesheng* is the insertion of *dou* and the relative order between *dou* and the polarity item.

Cheng and Giannakidou also argued that *dou* contributes to the maximality and exhaustivity of FCIs in Mandarin, as demonstrated by the contrast of the following two examples:

(21) Ta bu xiang mai na-ben-shu
He not want buy which-Cl-book
He doesn't want to buy *any* book (in particular)
(22) Ta na-ben-shu dou bu xiang mai.
He which-Cl-book *dou* not want buy
He doesn't want to buy *any* book (at all)

Example (22) has a very strong exhaustive reading, such that for a contextually determined set of books, 'he absolutely doesn't want any of them'. By contrast, in (21), the speaker is talking about a more general fact; there isn't a contextually salient set that is exhaustively evaluated.

How can we account for the contrast in degree of exhaustivity between these two sentences? I suggest that their difference can be explained in terms of the function of *dou* as a focus-sensitive and universal operator. More specifically, I will argue that it is the different meanings of the two distinct kinds of polarity items that cause exhaustivity to be present in one case and absent in the other. That is: (21) and (22) represent two typical licensing environments – for negative polarity items and FCIs, respectively. Based on this distinction, I conclude that it is not effective to rely on the exhaustivity of *dou* as a piece of evidence for the argument that *dou* is a maximality operator.

Cheng and Giannakidou (2005, 2013) weigh in on the function of *dou* in their investigation of FCIs in Chinese that seem to require the presence of *dou* in order to be licensed. They argued that *dou* contributes definiteness to Chinese FCIs, and that therefore it is natural to consider *dou* to be on a par with a definite determinerfunctioning as an iota/maximality operator. In subsequent work, Cheng and Giannakidou (2013) pursue this line of argument further, arguing that *dou* actually *is* a maximality operator. A pair of their examples is cited below:

(23) Ruguo (you) na-ge ren da-dianhua lai jiu shuo wo bu zai
 If have which-CL person telephone come then say I not be
 'if anyone calls, say that I'm not here.'
(24) (wulun) na-ge ren da-dianhua lai, wo dou bu zai
 no-matter which-CL person telephone come I am not be
 'Whoever calls, I'm not here.'

Sentence (23) is compatible with a situation where there is never actually a call received, while sentence (24) carries the expectation that somebody will eventually call. Building on this apparent existential contribution of *dou*, Cheng and Giannakidou (2013) introduce the following contrast to illustrate its exhaustivity contribution:

(25) Boling bu xiang jian na-ge ren
 Boling not want see which-CL person
 'Boling does not want to see *any* person (in particular).'
(26) Boling na-ge ren dou bu xiang jian
 Boling which-CL person all not want see
 'Boling does not want to see *any* person at all.'

Example (25) differs from (26) in that the former is compatible with the reading that there is no one in particular that Boling wants to see. This is, however, not a possible reading for the latter. Example (26) is only compatible with the reading that there is absolutely no one at all that Boling wants to see. I will argue that the exhaustivity introduced by the appearance of *dou* is not brought about by the function of *dou* as a maximality operator but as a universal quantifier with a tripartite structure. I will also argue that the existence effect arises because *dou* does not allow its restrictor to be empty.

Xiang (2008) similarly argues that, despite its different uses, the semantic core of *dou* remains the same: *dou* is simply a maximality operator. On Xiang's analysis, the different meanings of *dou* arise because that maximality is applied to different plural sets that are contextually determined. In other words, as a maximality operator, *dou* operates at the level of a set of covers, and its output is a maximal plural individual that consists of all the covers. Xiang used the following pair of sentences to illustrate this assessment:

(27) Haizimen qu-le gongyuan
 Children go-Perf Park
 The children went to the park.

(28) Haizimen dou qu-le gongyuan
Children *dou* go-Perf park
The children all went to the park.

In the contrast above, sentence (27) could be true if, for a large group of children, most of them went to the park, but one or two didn't. However, when *dou* is used, as shown in (28), the sentence can only be true if every child went to the park. Xiang thus argues that *dou* forces strong maximality. However, it's not clear that a maximality analysis does any better than a universality analysis or a distributivity analysis in accounting for the contrast in this pair of sentences. Furthermore, as I will show, an analysis that treats *dou* as an iota operator fails to account for any distributions that an analysis of *dou* as a universal adverb cannot explain, but also, the iota-operator analysis produces some wrong predictions for certain sentences containing *dou*.

According to Xiang, a contextually determined plural set may be a set of covers, a set of focus-induced alternatives or a set of degrees ordered on a scale. Among these three types of sets, the set of covers is the prototypical one. Yet, it is not actually possible to derive the correct meaning of a *dou* sentence by applying maximality to a set of covers. If we posit that *dou* is a maximality operator, we wind up over-predicting its meaning. To understand this, let's consider the definition of 'cover' provided by Schwarzschild (1996):

(29) A cover is a partition of the plurality P if and only if the following criteria are met:

C is a cover of P if and only if:

(1) C is a set of subsets of P
(2) Every member of P belongs to some set in C
(3) Φ is not in C

Based on this definition, Xiang proposed that *dou*, as a maximality operator, operates at the level of a set of covers and outputs a maximal plural individual that consists of all the covers. That is to say, *dou* applies the property denoted by the predicate to all the possible permutations and combinations of individuals contained within the denotation of the noun phrase quantified by *dou*.

However, the data suggest that *dou*'s quantificational power is not actually sufficient to achieve this. Consider the following example:

(30) Tamen dou shi yi gege de ren
They *dou* be one CL CLhuman being
'Each of them is a human being.'

Here, the word *yi* 'one' plus the reduplicated classifier *gege* expresses the meaning 'each individual'. However, on its surface, the predicate is singular ('be an individual'), while the subject *tamen* 'they' is plural. Thus, in this case, *dou* cannot possibly output a maximal plural individual that consists of all the covers of the set 'they'. Here is another example:

(31) Tamen dou shi fuqi
     They *dou* be couple
     'They are all couples.'

Suppose now that the set *tamen* has a denotation of Susan and Mike, Lynette and Tom (characters from the American television show *Desperate Housewives*). Because the predicate 'be a couple' can only be true for a pair of people, it can't be distributed over each single member of the set. The set has to be partitioned first.

In the case of the *Desperate Housewives* characters, we could have different ways to partition this set into smaller subsets. In other words, we could have different covers. The following are some of the possibilities:

(32) C1: {{S, M, L, T}}
     C2: {{S, M}, {L, T}}
     C3: {{S}, {M, L, T}}

     . . . . .

     Cn: {{S}, {M}, {L}, {T}}

It is obvious that, among these possibilities, the predicate 'be a couple' can only be applied to C2. Problematically, then, if we adopt Xiang's view that *dou* is a maximality operator that operates at the level of a set of covers and outputs a maximal plural individual that consists of all the covers, all the covers in (32) should be suitable for being couples! This is clearly not a convincing prediction.

It appears that, if (i) the concept 'cover' must be used and (ii) *dou* really is a maximality operator that operates at the level of a set of covers and outputs a maximal plural individual that consists of all the covers, Xiang's analysis can only predict the right meaning for sentences of the type shown below:

(33) Tamen dou shi pengyou
     They *dou* be friend
     'They are all friends.'

The predicate *shi pengyou* 'be friends' can be applied to all the covers of the set in question. That is, both the maximal plural individual that consists of all the pairs, plus all the other combinations of people, could all be friends.

Taking *dou* as a maximality operator also creates problems because it fails to predict a distributivity effect. For instance, if we take *dou* as a maximality operator, we must predict that '*abc* dou bought houses' asserts that 'the maximal element in the cover of *abc* bought houses', rather than that 'every element in the cover of abc bought houses'. Feng (2014) and Xiang (2016) have both talked a lot about this unreliability that arises when one takes *dou* as a maximality operator. To summarize, we have seen that this analysis can predict the interpretations of some *dou* sentences, but is unsatisfactory elsewhere: it fails to predict the interpretations of some *dou* sentences and sometimes even overpredicts others.

All the various readings of *dou* in the different sentences shown in (30), (31) and (33) depend on contextual factors and the semantic meanings of the predicates. The different readings of *dou* in these cases therefore seem most likely to arise due to the differences between relevant predicates. 'Be a couple' differs in a significant interpretive way from 'be friends' – and differs in a different way from 'be a human being', as well. The interpretation of the main verb 'be' depends on what kind of complement it takes. In the instance of 'be a couple', 'be' must have two individuals denoted by its subject, and denote a legal relationship. On the other hand, in the case of 'be friends', it is enough for two or more people to share friendship socially and emotionally, without any specification or restriction under the law. As to 'be a human being', this predicate carries a biological limitation as well as a restriction to independent individuals. Thus, how many individuals are taken into consideration in connection with a given predicate depends on that predicate's own semantic meaning. What *dou* does, however, is the same in all these various environments.

2.5 Different types of *dou*

The various functions of *dou* are given a unified account by Pan (2006), who analyzes *dou* in terms of its tripartite structure. The present book endorses the tripartite structure approach to *dou*. According to this approach, *dou* functions simply as a universal operator, which introduces a tripartite structure; the different meanings of *dou* are the result of different mapping mechanisms within this tripartite structure. More specifically, Pan (2006) proposes that *dou* is an adverb of universal quantification, which introduces a structure containing *dou* (as an operator) together with two unequal arguments, one of which serves as the restriction domain for the operator *dou* and the other of which serves as its nuclear scope.

In the previous sections, I introduced and critiqued the view that *dou* is a maximality or iota operator, as argued by Cheng and Giannakidou (2005) and Xiang (2008). In this section, I will follow Pan (2006), arguing that the various functions of *dou* can be best captured by understanding it as an operator that can introduce a tripartite structure to interpret the sentence containing it. After developing this hypothesis, I will present a comparison of the two approaches, showing the predictive power of each of them. Discovering what factor makes *dou* an effective licensor of Chinese polarity items is one of the ultimate goals of this research.

Following Pan (2006), I posit that *dou* can host the following types of tripartite structures:

(34) Left (universal) quantificational domain
   a   *dou* < phrase itself leftward (topic) > < nuclear scope rightward (comment) > unordered
   b   *dou* <ALT (topic focus)> <the sentence minus the focus> ordered
(35) Background quantificational domain
   c   *dou* < the rest of the sentence > <comment focus> unordered
   d   *dou* < the rest of the sentence > <comment focus> ordered

The examples which follow, taken from Pan (2006), illustrate these four possible types of *dou* sentences (A, B, C, D):

(36) a   Zhe xie shu ta *dou* kan guo le
         These book he *dou* read guo le
         'He has read all the books.'
         $\forall x[x \in [|\text{these books}|] \rightarrow$ he have read x]
   b   Ta *lian* shoutidiannao *dou* mai le
         He even notebook *dou* buy le
         'He even bought a notebook.'
         $\forall x[x \in \text{ALT (notebook)} \rightarrow$ he bought x]
   c   Ta *dou* xie de xiaoshuo
         He *dou* write de novel
         'All he wrote is novels.'
         $\forall x[\text{he wrote } x \rightarrow x=\text{novel}]$
   d   *Dou* daxuesheng le
         Dou college student
         '(Someone) has already become a college student.'
         $\forall x[\text{become } x \rightarrow x=\text{college student}]$

Among these different uses of *dou*, the left quantificational domain provides a set by itself, or introduces a set made up of focus alternatives for *dou* to quantify over as a universal operator. I call this type *universal quantification of dou;* in the next two subsections, I will compare this type with the *background quantification of dou*.

2.5.1 Universal quantification of dou

Although interpretations of *dou* seem to be complex, there are basically two major types of quantification at work: in the first type, *dou* is a universal quantifier with an non-empty set as its restriction domain; in the second type, *dou* is a focus-sensitive operator, and its restriction domain is provided by the background (i.e., the part of the sentence that isn't in focus). These two major types are demonstrated by (34) and (35). Let's first take a closer look at type (34) and try to unpack *dou*'s function of universal quantification.

44 Non-veridicality approach

There is a broad consensus in Chinese traditional linguistics supporting the proposal that *dou* is an adverb of quantification that functions to bestow universal quantification on some relevant noun phrase (see *Xiandai Hanyu Babaici* 'eight hundred words in modern Chinese' by Lü 1980). Consider the following examples:

(37) Chanpin dou yao jingguo zhiliang jiancha.
      product *dou* need undergo quality inspection
      'The quality of all the products needs to be checked on.'
(38) Wulun daxiao gongzuo, wo dou yao zuo hao.
      no-matter big-small work, we *dou* need do well
      'No matter whether the work is big or small, we need to do it very well.'

In these examples, the noun phrases that *dou* is quantifying are situated to its left; the quantified noun phrase can be bare, as in (37), or accompanied by *wulun* (meaning 'no matter' or 'regardless'), as in (38). The 'concession' meaning of *wulun* illustrated in (38) can also be expressed by *bulun* or *buguan* in Mandarin; for convenience, I will refer to all of these words under the label *wulun* in what follows.

No matter whether *wulun* is present or not, the phrase quantified by *dou* denotes a set with members without regard to order. For example, in (37), *dou* requires a quality inspection to be done with respect to all the products, regardless of status – the highest quality products, the second-best products and the low-quality products. It is this phrase to the left of *dou* that provides a restriction domain for the rightward predicate to operate within. The tripartite structure is shown as follows, together with its formal semantic interpretation:

(39) dou < products> <need to be undergo quality inspection >
      $\forall x[x \in [|\text{products}|] \rightarrow x$ needs to undergo quality inspection]

The quantification power of *dou* prevents the restriction domain from being empty; more specifically, it requires that the cardinality of the relevant members within this domain not be smaller than two. What will happen, then, if a single-member set or empty set occurs as the quantified phrase in the domain-restriction position of *dou*'s tripartite structure? Consider the following examples:

(40) *Taiyang dou hui faguang
      The sun *dou* can shine
      *'The sun all can shine.'
(41) ??Fenghuang dou zai yeli xianshen.
      Phoenix *dou* at night appear
      Intended: 'Phoenix all appears at night.'

We have no more than one sun in the real world, so the singular *taiyang* 'the sun' does not provide an acceptable plural set for *dou* to cover; as a result, the sentence in (40) is ungrammatical. As for the sentence in (41), the phoenix is an imaginary bird that does not exist in the real world; as a result, it is impossible to evaluate the sentence as true or false. Thus, as the universal quantification interpretation of *dou* predicts, neither the single-member set nor the empty set can provide a qualified restriction domain for *dou*. Note, however, that this does not mean that singular nouns are always ruled out of the quantified-object position in a *dou* sentence in Mandarin Chinese; *dou* can also quantify over the parts of an integral thing, as long as it is the parts that are discussed by the relevant predicate. A curious outcome of this behavior is that sentences with *dou* and the same singular noun may be grammatical in one case and ungrammatical in another:

(42) *Zhe tai diannao dou mai chuqu le
 This CL computer *dou* sell out le
 Intended: 'This computer has all been sold out.'
(43) Zhe tai diannao dou qingjie hao le.
 This CL computer *dou* clean finish le
 'The whole computer has been cleaned.'

The contrast above shows that *dou* requires more than one element to quantify over, but these elements may be members of the same type or of different types. A computer interpreted as a single entity (the form in which it will be sold) cannot occur in the domain restriction for *dou*, but when that same computer is viewed as a collection of parts (which must be cleaned one by one), its appearance in this context is perfectly licit. Thus, it is not strange that sentence (42) is ungrammatical whereas sentence (43) is totally okay.

Uncountable nouns can occur in the domain restriction of *dou* and be quantified over, since they either denote things that can be divided into more than one part or are regarded as being formed from more than one part. Consider the following example, where *shui* 'water' is a typical mass noun:

(44) Zheli de shui dou neng he
 Here de water *dou* can drink
 'All the water here can be drunk.'

The uncountable mass noun *shui* here satisfies the cardinality requirement of *dou*.

2.5.1.1 FCIs in concessive dou constructions

As noted above, the universal quantificational power of *dou* occurs not only in bare *dou* sentences, but also in sentences with an introductory concessive element such as *wulun* 'regardless of' or *lian* 'even'.

In constructions of the '*wulun* . . . *dou* . . .' type, the *wulun*-like element introduces a concessive clause. Consider the following sentences:

(45) Wulun yudao duoshao kunnan, wo dou yao kefu guoqu.
 No-matter meet more or less difficulty I *dou* will overcome over
 'I will overcome them no matter how many difficulties I encounter.'

(46) Wulun daxiao gongzuo, wo dou yao renzhen duidai
No-matter big small work, I *dou* will carefully treat
'I will treat it carefully no matter whether the work is big or small.'

In these sentences, we can see that the element that follows *wulun* may be a full clause or a noun phrase. In fact, a concessive clause introduced by *wulun* can be reduced to a nominal construction. See the following sentence, which is a simplified form of sentence (44):

(47) Wulun duoshao kunnan, wo dou yao kefu guoqu
No-matter more or less difficulty I *dou* will overcome over
'I will overcome them no matter how many difficulties I encounter.'

Looking closely, we can note an important similarity between the nominal *wulun*-constructions like (45) and (46). In both cases, the nominal elements – *duoshao kunnan* 'more or less difficulties' and *daxiao gongzuo* 'big or small works' – are vague and indefinite. The sets denoted by these noun phrases are unordered, or at least the order is obviously not emphasized. One important thing to emphasize here is that the set in question cannot be minimal; it must contain more than one member. Both these nominal elements could be considered FCIs from the perspective of polarity theory.

Although vague noun phrases like those shown previously are possible in *wulun*-constructions, the typical and most frequent noun phrases bound by *dou* in such sentences are indefinite *wh*-elements such as *shei* 'who', *shenme* 'what' and *na*-CL 'which'. Consider the sentences in (47), (48) and (49):

(48) Wulun shei dou yao zunshou falv.
No-matter who *dou* will obey law
'A person should obey the law, whoever he is.'
(49) Wulun shenme shiqing ta dou gan de feichang renzhen
No-matter what thing he *dou* do very carefully
'No matter what the thing is, he does it very carefully.'
(50) Wulun na-jian shi ta dou chuli de henhao
No-matter which-CL thing he *dou* deal de very well
'Whatever the thing is, he deals with it very well.'

This is a universal tendency for the meaning of free choice to be expressed by a concessive clause with a *wh*-element. Haspelmath (1997) argues that polarity items of this type are derived historically from concessive conditional clauses like that in (50) through a grammaticalization process in which the conditional clause is first reduced to an NP-plus-particle (see the intermediate step in (51)) and then becomes an argument of the main clause (see (52)). Consider the following Dutch examples, cited from Rullmann (1996):

(51) Niemand wil met een student spreken, welke student het ook is.
    no one wants with a student talk, which student it PRT PRT is
    'No one wants to talk to a student, whichever student it is.'
(52) Niemand wil spreken met een student, welke student dan ook.
    no one wants talk with a student, which student PRT PRT
    'No one wants to talk with a student, no matter which student.'
(53) Niemand wil spreken met welke student dan ook.
    no one wants talk with which student PRT PRT
    'No one want to talk with *any* student.'

These Dutch examples demonstrate the semantics of concessive conditionals. Rullmann argues that, intuitively, what the concessive clause in (51) does is to leave the choice of the student referred to in the main clause up to the hearer. The meaning of the sentence is something like the following: 'You, the hearer, may pick a student x; whatever choice you make, the proposition 'No one wants to talk to x' will be true'. Because it indicates that the choice of student is left up to the hearer, the concessive clause has the effect of strengthening the proposition expressed by the main clause. In other words, the function of the concessive clause is to strengthen the main clause by widening the potential denotation of the noun *student*. From a historical perspective, it seems, then, that the sort of semantics that Kadmon and Landman propose for *any* (see Chapter 1) is appropriate for *wh*-NPIs in Dutch.

Whatever the details of this grammaticalization process in Dutch may be, it is tempting to draw a similar connection between *wh*-polarity items in Mandarin and the concessive *wulun*-construction. Indeed, I believe that all Rullmann's arguments for Dutch may be suitably carried over to Mandarin. It's also important to note that, although Rullmann and Haspelmath refer to these types of polarity items as NPIs, they are really expressing free-choice meaning; in keeping with the terminology embraced in the rest of this study, I will call them FCIs (or, more generally, polarity items) in what follows.

'*Wulun . . . dou . . .*' constructions can be reduced to bare *dou* constructions; that is, it is always possible to omit *wulun*. Consider the following sentences:

(54) Shei dou yao zunshou falv
    who *dou* will obey law
    'People should obey the law whoever they are.'
(55) Shenme shiqing ta dou gan de feichang renzhen
    what thing he *dou* do very carefully
    'No matter what the thing is, he does it very carefully.'
(56) Na-jian shi ta dou chuli de henhao
    which-CL thing he *dou* deal de very well
    'Whatever the thing is, he deals with it very well.'

These sentences are the simplified forms of (48)–(50), without *wulun*. A few new questions can be raised here: are sentences with overt *wulun* always equivalent

48 *Non-veridicality approach*

in interpretation to the same sentences without *wulun*? Are there any contexts in which *wulun* cannot occur before the quantified noun phrases in (54)–(56)? Can we put any other elements in the position that *wulun* occupies?

There seem to be no quick and easy answers to these questions. Answering them may require digging deeper into the cardinality restrictions around this type of *dou* construction. Recall that noun phrases quantified by *dou* must not denote a set that is countable and has only one member. In other words, the noun phrase cannot be singular and cardinal. But it's unclear whether this same restriction holds true when a *wh*-element occurs in the domain restriction of *dou* – because it's as yet an open question whether *wh*-elements themselves are singular or plural. These questions about the distribution of *wulun* and the number features of polarity items are broad, and take us beyond the scope of the present book; I leave them to future study.

2.5.1.2 lian... dou... *constructions*

Both bare *dou* constructions and *wulun . . . dou . . .* constructions are of the (34) type. They quantify the noun phrase to the left side of *dou*. Notice that the quantified noun phrases in bare *dou* sentences and *wulun . . . dou . . .* sentences are not in focus – and in fact, sentences of this type in general do not have an obvious stress. If there is a stress, it always falls on *dou* itself. Setting aside these bare and *wulun*-type *dou* sentences, there are other two situations when focus does play an important role in the mapping of *dou*'s tripartite structure: in the first, focus falls on the element in topic position; in the second, focus falls on some element in the comment part of the sentence. In the former situation – when focus appears on the topic element – the restriction domain is the set of all the possible focus alternatives. In the latter situation – when focus falls on a comment element – the restriction domain is the background with respect to this focus. Any *dou* construction that bears a topic focus can also be phrased as a *lian . . . dou . . .* construction, where *lian* is glossed simply as 'even'. Consider the following examples:

(57) lian sansui xiaohai dou neng huida zhege wenti
even three years old kid *dou* can answer this question
'Even the kids of three years old can answer this question.'
(58) lian aizheng dou gei zhihao le
even cancer *dou* gei cure le
'Even cancer has been cured.'
(59) lian kuzi dou shi quanjiaren lunliu chuan
even pants *dou* be all the family in turn wear
'Even pants are taken by the family in turn.'

In *dou* sentences with this configuration, stress falls on the element between *lian* and *dou*, and this focused element denotes something extremely low in the hierarchy with respect to the discussion domain denoted by the predicate. Take sentence (58) for instance. Cancer is commonly recognized as one of the most terrible and difficult-to-cure ailments in modern medicine; as a result, it is situated on the bottom of the hierarchy of likely ailments for which a cure might be found. Since the alternatives to cancer are ordered with respect to how likely they are to be cured, and cancer is the least likely one, the statement that cancer has been cured entails that all lesser ailments (i.e., all the alternatives to cancer that are higher on the 'likelihood to be cured' hierarchy) have also been cured. In this way, universal quantification is obtained. See the tripartite structure and formal semantic analysis for this sentence below:

(60) Dou <ALT(cancer)> <can be cured>
(61) $\forall x[x \in ALT(cancer) \rightarrow x$ can be cured]

In the tripartite structure in (60) and the formal semantic analysis in (61), *dou*'s function is identical to its function in sentences of type (34). It is again a universal operator taking two arguments and making one argument (the nuclear scope) depends on the other (the restrictor). The sentence means that, for all disastrous things that are of the same type as cancer, they have been cured. Then what does *lian* do here? Type (34) differs from type (35) in how the restriction domain is determined. In the A type, the noun phrase serves as the restrictor straightforwardly, while in the B type, the relevant noun phrase simply provides a delimiter for the restriction domain by denoting an extreme member within it. *Lian* plays the role of placing this extreme element in focus, indicating that the restriction set contains all the members of the same type as (and less extreme than) this focused element.

Lian can be omitted from these sentences without changing the meaning. Consider the following examples, which show sentences equivalent to those in (57)–(59) without *lian*:

(62) sansui xiaohai dou neng huida zhege wenti
three years old kid dou can answer this question
'Even the kids of three years old can answer this question.'
(63) aizheng dou gei zhihao le
cancer dou gei cure le
'Even cancer has been cured.'
(64) yitiao kuzi dou shi quanjiaren lunliu chuan
one CL pants dou be all the family in turn wear
'Even pants are taken by the family in turn.'

There is no special stipulation on the number feature of the noun phrase following *lian*. It could be singular, as in (64), plural, as in (62) or uncountable, as in (44) and repeated in the following:

(65) Zheli de shui dou neng he.
here de water *d*ou can drink
'All the water here can be drunk.'

We can straightforwardly determine that these sentences are simplified forms of the *lian* ... *dou* ... construction (rather than bare *dou* constructions) by checking the sentence intonation. Take sentence (62) for instance. If the noun phrase in the topic position, *sansui xiaohai* 'kids of three years old', receives stress (and is therefore in focus), this sentence must be derived from a *lian* ... *dou* ... construction; it receives the interpretation that this question is so easy that nearly everyone can answer it. If the sentential stress instead falls on *dou* itself, this sentence is derived from a bare *dou* construction, and receives the interpretation that all the kids of three years old can answer this question (without carrying any information about how people older or younger than three years old will do).

Based on this data, I conclude that the noun phrase in *lian* ... *dou* ... constructions must have some kind of scalar meaning; that is, it denotes the top or bottom member of an ordered set. If *shenme* and *na*-CL also have a scalar meaning, then the alternative sets of them (that is, all members of the same ordered set of which the *wh*-word denotes the top or bottom member) will satisfy the restriction of *dou*. Consider the example below:

(66) Shenme shu ta dou kan guo le
    What book he dou read guo le
    'He has read all the books.'

If *shenme shu* 'what books' can be considered to have a scalar meaning, in which it denotes the least likely book he could have read, the restriction of *dou* will be the alternative set of *shenme shu* – that is, the various books he could possibly read. This is captured by the following formal semantic analysis:

(67) $\forall x[x \in \text{ALT(shenme shu)} \rightarrow \text{he has read } x]$

The question is whether this interpretation, where the restriction domain is a set of alternatives to *shenme shu*, is meaningfully different from the more straightforward interpretation, where the restriction domain is the set of all books denoted by *shenme shu* directly. The number feature of *shenme* provides the key to answering this question. Specifically, *shenme shu* can only be singular (by its nature). As a result, it cannot directly serve as the restrictor for *dou* – since, as we saw, the cardinality requirement for quantification under *dou* disallows a situation where there is only one member in the domain restriction. Thus, the interpretation of this sentence must follow the alternative-set type.

The situation with *na*-CL, too, is made easier to interpret thanks to its singular number. *Na*-CL introduces an alternative set, which is plural and serves as the restriction domain of *dou*; again, we know this is the case because if *na*-CL NP alone were interpreted as the domain restriction, this would violate the cardinality requirement of *dou*'s quantification in type (34). Conversely, in the '*lian* ... *dou* ...' type, the alternatives are scalable and the focus is on one end of the relevant scale. Thus, if a *na*-CL noun phrase is licensed in type (34), it must be interpreted as the element at the top or the bottom of a scale. This prediction aligns with the analyses put forward by Lee and Horn (1994); Kadmon and Landman (1993) and others in the literature: according to these authors, polarity items such as *any* in English denote 'indefinite, plus some additional meaning'. The 'plus' component in Lee and Horn (1994) is the end-of-scale semantics associated with *even*; in Kadmon and Landman (1993), it is a combination of their notions of contextual widening and logical strengthening.

The fact that *na*-CL noun phrases are inherently singular is sufficient to exclude their involvement in bare *dou* constructions. However, it still remains undetermined whether these singular *na*-CL noun phrases are underlyingly *lian... dou...* constructions or *wulun... dou...* constructions. The crucial key to the question is whether they express scalar meaning or indiscriminate meaning. A goal of this study is to determine whether or not polarity items have scalar meaning in Mandarin.

One important point to note is that some *na*-CL noun phrases do, in fact, appear in bare *dou* constructions. Consider the following sentence:

(68) Na-ban de xuesheng dou jige le?
      Which class de student dou pass le
      'Which class of students all passes the examination?'

Neither *wulun* nor *lian* can precede *na*-CL in the sentence above; this is unequivocally an illustration of a bare *dou* construction. However, this is not a problem for my analysis, since this sentence can only express an interrogative meaning. That is to say, *na* here is not an FCI, but an interrogative element. The cardinality requirement of the bare *dou* construction is therefore satisfied by the classifier rather than *na* itself. *Ban* 'class' is a collective noun and serves as a collective classifier in sentence (68). The number of students in a class is generally bigger than one, therefore meeting the requirement of the bare *dou* construction perfectly adequately.

2.5.1.3 suoyou... dou... *constructions*

In each of the three *dou* constructions we have examined so far, *dou* cooperates with a different element: *lian, wulun* or an empty introducing element. Questions follow naturally: does the bare *dou* construction have a full form like *lian... dou...* and *wulun... dou...* constructions do? And, if so, then why do we define it as a 'bare' *dou* construction?

In fact, bare *dou* sentences do have a full form in Mandarin. However, interestingly, the element that appears in this full form is not a function word like *lian* or *wulun*, but a substantive one: the adjective *suoyou(de)*, meaning 'all' or 'entire'. Consider the following examples:

(69) (suoyoude) xuesheng dou tongguo le zhege kaoshi
      All students dou pass le this exam
      'All the students passed this exam.'

(70) (suoyoude) laoshi dou nadao le jiaoshi zigezheng
All teacher dou get le teach certificate
'All the teachers got the certificate of teaching.'

These examples show that *souyou* makes no extra, exceptional contribution to the bare *dou* construction; it adds nothing new. The universal quantificational power of these sentences is entirely obtained from *dou*, and all *suoyou* does is to repeat and reinforce it. In contrast, both *lian* and *wulun* have their own characteristics independent of *dou*. *Lian* adds emphasis to the domain restrictor by highlighting its relationship within a hierarchical scale; it means 'even'. The focus effect it introduces allows *dou* to get its domain restriction through focus association. *Wulun* is a concessive element that introduces a concessive clause. The *wh*-noun phrase in the *wulun* . . . *dou* . . . construction are the subject or object of that concessive clause. Since *suoyou* brings nothing new to bare *dou* constructions, there is no need to define them as *suoyou* . . . *dou* . . . constructions.

2.5.1.4 (Wulun) shenme dou vs. (suoyou) shenme dou

We know that all three types of *dou* sentences can omit their respective introducing element and become a seemingly bare *dou* sentence:

(71) (')Wulun   A   dou   B
(72) (')Suoyou   A   dou   B
(73) Lian   'A   dou   B

These three types of sentences can be classified into different groups, depending on one's perspective. For instance, the final type (*lian* . . . *dou* . . .) is different from the first two types from the perspective of information structure or focus arrangement. Focus always falls on the scalar element between the two elements *lian* and *dou* in *lian* . . . *dou* . . . sentences, whereas there is generally no obvious sentential stress (and therefore no focus) in sentences containing *wulun* . . . *dou* or (*suoyou* . . .) *dou*. Even when stress does occur, it falls on the introducing element in both types of structures. So, it is easy to tell *lian* . . . *dou* . . . constructions apart from the other two types based on an assessment of its stress.

In addition to the hint provided by stress, the properties of the noun phrase preceding *dou* (noun phrase A, in the schematic above) can also help listeners distinguish the *lian* . . . *dou* . . . type from the other two types. Given the characteristics of *lian* . . . *dou* . . . constructions, listeners should expect the A element between *lian* and *dou* to be some kind of scalar. More specifically, this element should bear some end-of-scale meaning, similar to what Horn (2000) described for freechoice and negative polarity *any*. In the Mandarin Chinese context, for instance, it is possible to predict that all minimizers (such as *yi-fen qian* 'one cent', *ban-ge ren* 'half a person') will be able to appear between *lian* and *dou* very naturally. Take the following sentences, for example:

(74) (Lian) yi-fen qian dou you jiazhi
Even one CL money dou have value
'Even one cent has its own value.'
(75) (Lian) ban-ge ren dou bu neng yang huo
Even half-CL person dou not can feed live
'Even half a person cannot be fed.'

Minimizers are (usually idiomatic) polarity items referring to minimal quantities that are the symbolic lowest points of some scale. Typical examples in English include *a red cent* and *(to drink) a drop*. In Mandarin Chinese, some of these kinds of *lian . . . dou . . .* sentences with minimizers have actually been frozen into four-syllable idioms, such as *yi-wen-bu-ming* (meaning 'having no money at all') and *hao-fa-wu-sun* (meaning 'not being hurt at all').

A very frequently used polarity item in Mandarin is *renhe*. Since *renhe* already has a concessive element *ren* (meaning *wulun* 'regardless of') at the morphological level, *renhe* is excluded from *lian . . . dou . . .* sentences. Then, the next question is: how do bare *wh*-indeterminates and *na*-CL polarity items behave in terms of denoting scalar meaning? Are they capable of denoting scalar end-points, or are they just indiscriminate, providing no specific information about the order of the noun phrases that follow them? These questions will be left for future work.

So, it is clear how to distinguish *lian . . . dou . . .* sentences from the other two types of *dou* constructions. What can be more difficult is separating *wulun . . . dou . . .* constructions from *(suoyou . . .) dou . . .* constructions, since they cannot be distinguished on the basis of their pronouncing stress alone, and their introducing elements *suoyou* and *wulun* are not always overt. Often, it is necessary to rely on other hints, such as the number feature of the element before *dou*, to tell these two types apart. This distinction will be important as we move forward in this study, since distinguishing between all three types of *dou* sentences is a crucial step in understanding the real licensing factor for Chinese polarity items sanctioned in *dou* sentences.

2.5.2 Background quantificational domain of dou

In those cases where Mandarin *wh*-polarity items *can* occur with *dou*, they always appear before it in the linear structure. *Wh*-elements that occur after *dou* are not polarity items, but interrogative words. Let's now take a look at *dou* constructions of types (34) and (35), which show a different distribution then the universal quantification *dou* constructions discussed above.

When a focus element occurs in the comment of a sentence with *dou*, the mapping of the tripartite structure introduced by *dou* is determined by the focus – background structure rather than topic – comment structure. The focused element in the comment is interpreted as the nuclear scope of *dou*, while the restriction domain is the background – that is, the whole sentence minus the focus element.

See the following examples, where *daxuesheng* 'college student' in sentence (76) and *gonghe* 'being a republic country' in sentence (77) are stressed:

(76) ni dou daxuesheng le, zenme zheme jiandan de daoli dou bu dong
you *dou* college le how so easy principle *dou* understand
'You have already been a college student, so how do you not understand this easy principle?'
(77) Zhongguo dou gonghe le, Yuan Shikai haiyao dang huangding
China *dou* republic le Yuan Shikai still want act king
'China had become a republic, yet Yuan Shikai still wanted to act as the king of China.'

Their corresponding tripartite structures and formal semantic interpretations can be deconstructed as follows:

(78) a   dou <you become x> <x=college student>
 b $\forall x$[you become x $\rightarrow$ x=college student]
(79) a   dou <China become x> <x = republic state>
 b $\forall x$[China become x $\rightarrow$ x = republic state]

It is, of course, easier for college students than kids of three years old to understand certain principles. The focus on *daxuesheng* 'college students' introduces a set of alternatives, such as high school students, primary school students, kindergarteners and even little babies. Generally speaking, in this domain of all students (or children) of different intelligence levels, the focus element *daxuesheng* is the highest one. As for the story of *Yuan Shikai*, he was a warlord in the history of China, and he wanted to be the king even when the country had changed from a feudal state to a republic state. Maybe his behavior would have been less unforgivable if the country had still been on its way to republicanism from feudalism. By placing the focus on *gonghe* 'republic', the speaker emphasizes that it is worse to wish to be king in this context than the alternatives, which form an ordered set with *gonghe* on the extreme end.

Type (35) also has another subtype, which differs from the one illustrated earlier in that its domain restriction is provided by a set of unordered members:

(80) Ta dou chuan [mianzhi]$_F$ yifu
He *dou* wear cotton clothes
'All he wears is cotton clothes.'
(81) Ta dou kan xie [meiyong de]$_F$ dongxi
He *dou* read some useless de thing
'All he reads is something useless.'

In sentence (80), the singular personal pronoun *ta* 'he' by itself cannot provide a sufficient domain restriction for *dou*. In addition, applying the alternatives of 'he' as the domain restriction is also not possible, because focus falls within the comment part of the sentence, rather than on the domain restrictor itself. Observe that stress is marked on *mianzhi* 'cotton', an element whose peer members include fur, leather, wool and other materials. The sentence means that, among all these different garment materials, he always wears cotton clothes. Though cotton is focused here, the other possible garment materials are disordered with respect to a specific personal preference. In a similar way, the restriction domain of *dou* in (81) contains members out of order. All *dou* does is to give a domain that limits the predicate, and then pick one member from it (see the tripartite structure and formal semantic interpretation below).

(82) a   dou <he read x > <x = useless things>
     b $\forall x[\text{he read } x \rightarrow x = \text{useless things}]$

The function of *dou* in type (35) is similar to the function of the Mandarin adverb *zhi* 'only'. The sentences in (80) and (81) can be paraphrased as follows:

(83) ta zhi chuan mianzhi yifu
     he only wear cotton clothes
     'He only wears cotton clothes.'
(84) ta zhi kan xie meiyong de dongxi
     he only read some useless de thing
     'He only reads some useless things.'

The semantics of *zhi* 'only' says: no proposition from the set of relevant contrasts other than the one expressed by its syntactical sister sentence α is true. *Zhi* also carries an additional implicature that α is in fact true. The corresponding formal semantics of (83) and (84) are:

(85) $\forall x[\text{he wears } x \rightarrow x = \text{cotton clothes}]$
(86) $\forall x[\text{he read } x \rightarrow x = \text{something useless}]$

The semantic interpretations above also match the interpretation of the *dou* sentences in (80) and (81). This evidence supports the analysis of Horn (1996), who argues that there exists a converse relation between 'only' and 'all', recognized since medieval times:

(87) 'Tantum animal est homo convertitur in istam: omnis homo est animal, peristam regulam: Exclusiva affirmativa convertitur in universalem P'.
(88) only (A, B) (only As are Bs) ↔ all Bs are As ↔ B⊆A

Sentence (87), which means 'the only animal is man' (only animals are humans), is converted to the interpretation 'every human is (an) animal' by a rule which states that an affirmative exclusive is equivalent to a universal.

56   *Non-veridicality approach*

Though *zhi* and *dou* are not the exact counterparts of *only* and *all* in English, the two elements in Mandarin are exchangeable in the situation summarized in type (35). The close relationship and mutual derivation between *zhi* and *dou* will shed light on our investigation of *dou*. In particular, when we come to investigate *dou*'s property of focus sensitivity, this previous research on the focus association of *zhi* and *only* will be very useful.

This subsection has examined *dou*'s quantification when the domain restriction is provided by the focus background; although it may seem like this discussion has little to do with our main topic, the connection will soon become clear. To see why, let us next consider whether *wh*-polarity items can be licensed in this type of *dou* construction. First, let's consider whether *wh*-elements can appear before *dou* in constructions of type (35):

(89)   shei dou chuan [mianzhi yifu]$_F$?
       Who *dou* wear cotton clothes
       'Who always wear cotton clothes?'
(90)   Na-ge ren dou chuan [mianzhi yifu]$_F$?
       Which ge man dou wear cotton clothes
       'Which man always wears cotton clothes?'

These two sentences are interrogatives, and their focus is in the comment part. Since the interrogative meaning must be attributed to the bare *wh*-element *shenme* 'what' and the *wh*-element *na* 'which', we must conclude that these two *wh*-elements are not polarity items – they do not express either negative polarity or free choice. When equivalent sentences end in declarative punctuation, they are ungrammatical. Thus, it appears that *wh*-polarity items cannot appear in the topic part of a *dou* construction of type (35).

Then what about the comment part? Consider the following examples:

(91)   Ta dou chuan shenme yifu?
       He *dou* wear what clothes
       'What does he always wear?'
(92)   Ta dou chuan na-zhong yifu?
       He *dou* wear which kind clothes
       'Which kind of clothes does he always wear?'

The situation is similar with the previous one. *Wh*-elements can appear in the comment part in this type of sentence, but they can only express their interrogative meaning. Again, *wh*-polarity items such as *shenme* and *na*-CL are entirely ruled out of the nuclear scope of *dou*.

In fact, what these sections show is that the locations where *wh*-polarity items are licensed in *dou* sentences are all downward-entailing environments. This downward entailment is best attested in the domain restriction, rather than the nuclear scope, of universal quantifiers. As a result, *wh*-polarity items can be naturally licensed in the domain restriction of a universal operator *dou*, as in constructions of type (34). On the other hand, they cannot be licensed in the domain restriction of a tripartite structure when focus falls on the comment part. Intriguingly, however, another polarity item, *conglai* 'ever', *can* occur in this environment. I will offer further insight into these observations.

This chapter introduces the non-veridicality approach to polarity items. I focus in particular on the work of Cheng and Giannakidou (2005, 2013), which interprets Chinese polarity items as intensionalized elements that can only be licensed in non-veridical contexts. I then present an overview of several previous studies which present conclusive evidence that the non-veridical approach is insufficient to explain Chinese polarity sensitivity. I highlight the characteristics of the pre-*dou* position as being particularly problematic for the non-veridicality approach, and then argue against the proposal that *dou* is a maximality operator. The discussion in this chapter sets up the question addressed in the next chapter: what is the essential role of *dou* in licensing polarity items?

3 Tripartite structure and *dou*

As the past two chapters have shown, *dou* sentences are crucial to the analysis of polarity items. Episodic *dou* sentences that contain negative polarity or free-choice items (NPIs or FCIs) constitute counterexamples to the non-veridicality approach to polarity items, but they cannot be dealt with entirely straightforwardly under the downward-entailing approach either. The reason that these kinds of sentences are grammatical is an outstanding problem, and one of the main questions this study will attempt to address.

In the last chapter, I introduced Pan's (2006) work on *dou*. This study builds on the groundwork laid by Pan (2006) by continuing to apply the tripartite structural framework to the analysis of *dou* in Mandarin. This approach is appealing because it allows us to create a direct link between the presence of *dou* and the existence of a downward-entailment reading; as we have already seen, this is an obligatory condition for some Mandarin polarity items, and downward entailment is already a cross-linguistically acknowledged licensing condition for polarity items. Below, I repeat the two major types of tripartite structures that can be introduced by *dou*:

- Left quantificational domain
  a   dou<phrase itself leftward (topic) ><nuclear scope rightward (comment)> unordered
  b   dou<ALT (topic focus)><the sentence minus the focus> ordered
- Background quantificational domain
  c   *dou*< the rest of the sentence ><comment focus> unordered
  d   *dou*< the rest of the sentence ><comment focus> ordered

It should be emphasized that these tripartite structures do not necessarily represent the full linguistic structure of the corresponding sentences; instead, they represent some properties that these sentences have in common. What, then, is the definition of tripartite structure, and what is the essential generalization captured by the tripartite structure approach to *dou*? I will address these questions in the following sections.

3.1 Asymmetry of the two arguments

To date, in the linguistics literature, no scholar has proposed an accurate definition or conclusive diagnostic treatment for the notion of tripartite structure. According to Hajičová, Partee and Sgall (1998), however, two properties appear to play a central role in the cases that are most frequently analyzed in terms of tripartite structure. Constructions with these two properties seem to form some kind of natural class with the strong quantifiers.

One property that is crucial for the 'essential tripartite structure' (per Partee and Sgall) is that the 'operator' be semantically a function that takes two arguments and treats them differently – i.e., a non-symmetrical function. Thus, for example, a simple conjunction operator – assuming it is properly symmetrical in its two arguments – could not give rise to a tripartite structure in this 'true' sense. Given this premise, let us consider the case of *dou*. *A dou B* and *B dou A* are not semantically identical at all:

(1) Haoshu dou shi dajia xihuan de shu
    Good book all be everyone like de book
    'All good books are books that are liked by everyone.'
(2) Dajiaxihuan de shu dou shi haoshu
    Everyone like de book all be good book
    'All the books that everyone likes are good books.'

The prior two sentences do not have the same meaning; after all, we all know of many cases where good books and best-sellers are not identical. For a weaker quantifier like *at least three*, on the other hand, the situation is different. *At least three As are Bs* is semantically equal to *at least three Bs are As*. Consider the following example, with *zhishao* meaning 'at least' in Mandarin:

(3) (zhe-ge ban) zhishao san-gexiaohaishi Xizang ren
    This class at least three children be Tibetan
    'At least three children (in this class) are Tibetan.'
(4) (zhe-ge ban) zhishao san-ge xizangren shi xiaohai
    This class at least three-CL Tibetan be children
    'At least three Tibetans (in this class) are children.'

Though the two sentences above are not identical, they are closely related in meaning. So, in this case, as well, *at least three* cannot be analyzed in terms of tripartite structure, as *dou* and *every* can. This asymmetry, according to Partee (1987), is a central property of 'essentially quantificational' determiners, and plays a central role in the interpretation of noun phrases and their type-shifting principles.

3.2 Conservativity of the two arguments

The second property borne by elements with tripartite structure is the property of conservativity. The principle of conservativity is consistent with the idea that one of the arguments of the tripartite structure should be a 'domain restrictor'. The notion 'conservativity' is defined as follows in Partee and Sgall:

(5) An operator O which applies to two sets A and B is conservative on its first argument if O (A, B) is necessarily equivalent to O (A, A∩B).

That is, if O is an operator conservative on its first argument A, then the only part of its second argument B that needs to be taken into account is that subset of B which is also in A; nothing outside of set A will be relevant to the truth condition of the whole. For such an operator, it makes sense to call A its domain argument or restrictor. I propose that *dou* is such a conservative operator, and that the relationship between *dou*'s two arguments is that of a delimiter and a dependent thing. Consider the following example:

(6) xianggangchengshidaxue de xuesheng biye qian dou bixu xuehui youyong.
    City University of Hong Kong de student graduate before *dou* must learn swim
    'All the students of City University of Hong Kong must learn how to swim before they graduate.'

In the sentence above, the conversation range is limited to students of City University of Hong Kong. Whether or not the students of other universities or colleges must learn how to swim does not fall within the scope of the sentence and is not relevant to its truth condition. Since passing the swimming test is a requirement for students of City University of Hong Kong, sentence (6) is true.

The definition of conservativity given above needs to be generalized in some way if it is to be applicable to operators whose arguments do not both belong to the same type of set. As it turns out, the conservative property can be straightforwardly extended to some other types of operators, and can be putatively extended to some others. To begin with, let's check *dou*'s conservativity again by analyzing sentence (7) in terms of the definition of conservativity.

(7) Zhongguoren dou yinggai henhao de zhangwo hanyu.
    Chinese *dou* should very well de master Chinese
    'All Chinese people should master Chinese very well.'

For a sentence like (7), the three parts in the definition of conservativity (O, A and B) are represented by *dou* (O), the set of all Chinese people (A), and the set of people who should master the Chinese language well (B). If the universal quantifier *dou* is really an operator that is conservative on its first argument, the following statement should be true, based on the definition of conservativity laid out in (5):

(8) Dou (all Chinese people, the set of members who should master Chinese)
    = *dou* (all Chinese people, all Chinese people ∩ the set of members who should master Chinese)

This equation is an informal abstraction, of course; in order to check if it is true or false, it's helpful to translate it into a formal representation:

(9) $\forall x\ [x \in \text{Chinese people} \rightarrow x \text{ should master Chinese}]$
    $= \forall x\ [x \in \text{Chinese people} \rightarrow x \in \text{Chinese people and } x \text{ should master Chinese}]$

(10) If x = p, then:
   If p is a Chinese person, then p should master Chinese.
   = If x = p: if p is a Chinese person, then p is a Chinese person and p should master Chinese.

The logical equivalence in (10) illustrates that (9) is true, and the truth of (9) guarantees the validity of the equation in (8). From this argument, we can see that *dou* is an operator that is conservative on its first argument; as such, it meets the second property for a class operator, and therefore deserves to be singled out for attention under the rubric of tripartite structures.

Using the tripartite structure to analyze *dou* offers a satisfying explanation for the cardinality requirement of its restrictor: the principle of conservativity requires that the first argument (A) of *dou* cannot be an empty set. How come? If A is empty, then it has no members for B to depend on. This circumstance, in turn, leads to the result that it is impossible to determine whether B is true or false. This makes sense from an intuitive standpoint: rationally, an operator that carries the property of so-called conservativity must have something to conserve. Being the case, it should come as no particular surprise that empty or null As are ruled out as candidates for *dou*'s restrictor.

3.3 Conservativity in *if*-clauses and *wulun* ... *dou* ... constructions

In the view of Heim (1982), *if*-clauses in English always have the semantic role of serving as (parts of) restrictor clauses to operators in tripartite structures. Given that this is their inherent role, we can say that *if*-clauses naturally belong to the class of constructions that can be written as tripartite structures. The antecedent clause of an *if*-construction contributes to the domain relative to which the main clause (the nuclear scope) is interpreted. For illustration, let's take a look at the tripartite structure in (13) and its natural-language equivalents in English (*if-then* sentence, (11)) and Chinese (*ruguo* ... *name* ... sentence, (12)):

(11) If trees are green, then small trees are green.
(12) Ruguoshushilvse de, name xiaoshuyeshilvse de.
   If tree be green de, then small tree also be green de
(13) if/then (trees are green, small trees are green)
   $\forall x$ [$x \in$ trees & x is green $\rightarrow$ $x \in$ small trees & x is green]

If the *ruguo* ... *name* ... construction in Mandarin, like English *if*-constructions, fits into the semantic interpretation captured by tripartite structure, it follows that the *wulun* ... *dou* ... construction in Mandarin should also fit this interpretation, since the *wulun* ... *dou* ... construction can be analyzed as a serial variant of the *ruguo* ... *name* ... construction. Consider the *wulun* ... *dou* ... sentence in (14) and the series of *ruguo* ... *name* ... sentences in (15), which elaborate its meaning:

(14) wulun ni shi shei, dou bixu zunshou falü
   no-matter you be who, *dou* must obey law
   'No matter who you are, you must obey the law.'

(15) a   ruguo ni shi guowang, ni bixu zunshou falü
         if you be king you must obey law
         'If you are the king, you must obey the law.'
     b   *ruguo* ni shi shizhang, ni bixu zunshou falü
         if you be mayor you must obey law
         'If you are the mayor, you must obey the law.'
     c   *ruguo* ni shi zhangsan lisi, ni bixu zunshou falü
         if you be Tom, Dick or Harry you must obey law
         'If you are Tom, Dick or Harry, you must obey the law. '
     d   ...
     e   ...

Based on the relationship between the sentence in (14) and the sentences in (15), we can see that what we are actually dealing with in a *wulun . . . dou . . .* construction is a group of related *ruguo . . . name . . .* sentences. In other words, concessive clauses are essentially conditionals.

Tracing this relationship between concessives and conditionals should draw to mind the case of the Dutch concessive clauses we saw in the last chapter. The Dutch examples are shown here:

(16) Niemand wil met een student spreken, welke student het ook is.
     no one wants with a student talk, which student it PRT PRT is
     'No one wants to talk to a student, whichever student it is.'
(17) Niemand wil spreken met een student, welke student dan ook.
     no one wants talk with a student, which student PRT PRT
     'No one wants to talk with a student, no matter which student.'
(18) Niemand wil spreken met welke student dan ook.
     no one wants talk with which student PRT PRT
     'No one want to talk with *any* student.'

These Dutch examples demonstrate the semantics of concessive conditionals. Recall that, in that case, the speaker of the clause left the specifics of the interpretation up to the hearer to imagine. In using his imagination to flesh out the meaning of the sentence, the hearer is actually dealing with a series of *if*-conditionals. For example, in (14), following Rullmann, we may understand the speaker to be saying the following: 'You, the hearer, may pick a human being x; whatever choice you make, the proposition 'x must obey the law' will be true'. The choice of human beings is left to the hearer, who will make the choice by checking the validity of the statement against a group of conditional sentences he creates by himself. A new conditional sentence is created each time the hearer assigns a value to x. The number of assignments to x equals to the number of conditional sentences. In other words, the function of the concessive clause is to consider all the possibilities of the main clause by widening the potential denotation of the relevant noun phrases, including the *wh*-elements.

In the case of obedience to the law described in the Mandarin example previously, the free-choice meaning of the *wh*-element derives, in some sense from all the conditionals implied by the concessive clauses. That is one choice, one conditional. To state it in another way, the range of choices available is as broad as the range of available, relevant conditionals. When the speaker uses the *wulun* . . . *shei* . . . *dou* . . . construction to express her view on what kinds of people must obey the law, she indicates to the hearer that he should pick as many candidates as possible for *shei*, and even marginal choices can be taken into consideration. Each candidate the hearer chooses introduces a new conditional, which the speaker claims will be true based on the judgment of the hearer.

So, what is the main point of this subsection, given that the primary focus of this study concerns the treatment of NPIs/FCIs in Mandarin? In the paragraphs above, I devoted some space to prove that *wulun* . . . *dou* . . . constructions are essentially conditionals, just like *ruguo* . . . *name* . . . construction in Mandarin and *if* . . . *then* . . . sentences in English. This means that, like a *ruguo*-clause, a *wulun*-clause introduces a restriction domain for the main clause. The two arguments of *dou* thus must have a conservativity relationship – which, as we have discussed, is one of two crucial properties shared by all constructions with a tripartite structure. Here is an illustration of the tripartite structure of the *wulun* . . . *dou* . . . sentence in (14):

(19) wulun/dou (you are x, x must obey the law)
(20) $\forall x$[you are x $\rightarrow$ x must obey the law]

In the tripartite structure in (19), the nuclear component 'x must obey the law' depends on the restrictor 'you are x'. That is to say: the x who must obey the law is the x you are. If there is a y and you are not y, then the question of whether or not y must obey the law is beyond the scope of the sentence. So, although the domain of x is certainly widened by the *wulun* . . . antecedent clause, it still has to be possible for you to be a member of that domain. This imposes certain natural limitations: for instance, if both the speaker and the hearer (denoted by 'you' in the ongoing conversation) know the hearer is female, then it is nonsense for the hearer to assign a male value to x. It is for this reason that sentence (14) is not totally equivalent to the following sentence, where the restriction domain is provided straightforwardly by a plural noun phrase:

(21) Suoyou de ren dou bixu zunshou falv.
All de person *dou* must obey law
'Everyone must obey the law.'

Suoyou de ren means 'all the people' or 'everyone'. The tripartite structure and format is the following:

(22) dou (human beings, must obey the law)
(23) $\forall x$[x$\in$human beings $\rightarrow$ x must obey the law]

The interpretation in (23) is different from (20) in how the variable x is restricted. In the bare *dou* sentence, x is a member of the set denoted by the noun phrase that precedes *dou*. A member of the set of all human beings is of course a human being. On the other hand, in the *wulun . . . dou . . .* sentence, x is a member of the set containing all the possible *you*s. If this set is gathered by name, then x could be Tom, Dick or Harry. If this set is organized by social status, then x could be a king, an officer or a beggar. And there always exists the possibility that this set may contain all the factors that determine or define a human being. In the restriction domain of *dou* under this situation, *wulun ni shi shei* 'no matter who you are' is semantically identical to *suoyuo ren* 'all the people'. Thus, we can see that the *wulun . . .* antecedent clause can limit the utterance to a conversational scope, while the bare *dou* clause (plus a plural noun phrase) cannot limit the utterance in this way, even though both types of clauses can serve as the restriction domain of a tripartite structure.

3.4 Other issues under the frame of tripartite structure

As Heim noted, it is not only determiner quantifiers and adverbial quantifiers that can be analyzed in terms of operator, restrictor and nuclear scope. Modal verbs, and even negation, display many of the same properties, suggesting strongly that their logical structures also involve a principal argument, an unclear scope and another argument, which provides a restriction domain over which they quantify or otherwise 'operate'.

It should be emphasized that, in all of these instances, the proposed tripartite structure does not necessarily represent *the only available* linguistic structure for these constructions; rather, it represents some properties that these construction shave in common. I use the tripartite structure primarily as a helpful construct to guide our discussion concerning generalizations shared by certain classes of constructions that involve quantificational (or quantification-like) operators. Sentences containing no quantifiers, and no *if*-clauses or other relevant operators, are assumed to have a 'simplex' rather than tripartite structure.

So far in this section, I have used the tripartite structure to analyze bare *dou* constructions and *wulun . . . dou . . .* constructions. In the linguistics literature, it is English adverbs of quantification like *always* and *usually* that are the prototypical cases that are analyzed in this way. However, the phenomenon seems to be much broader, and may extend to a number of other types of operators. Table 3.1, borrowed from Hajičová, Partee and Sgall (1998),[1] lists some of these potential operators, showing the scope of tripartite structure:

(24)

Table 3.1

OP	RESTRICTOR	NUCLEAR SCOPE
	Background	Focus (content including focus)
	Alternatives	Chosen alternatives
	Context	Context-dependent content
	Domain	Nuclear scope
	Preconditions	Assertion

OP	Antecedent (anchors)	Anaphors
	Topic	Comment
	If-clause	Main clause
	...	...
	RESTRICTOR	NUCLEAR SCOPE

Partee and Sgall acknowledge that not all of the listed cases have been analyzed in terms of tripartite structure in existing works; as a result, they point out that this diagram must be regarded as speculative and in many respects still rather vague – almost metaphorical. Nevertheless, this generalized table is very important for the purposes of the present study, because it successfully captures the essential spirit of the distribution of Chinese *wh*-polarity items. As shown in the summary diagram of Table 3.1, in addition to *dou* sentences, *ruguo . . . name . . . (if . . . then . . .*) sentences and modal sentences can also be interpreted using tripartite structure – and they all turn out to be appropriate environments for non-interrogative *shenme, shei* and *na*-CL NPs.

3.5 The mapping mechanism of tripartite structures

In analyzing *dou* sentences, it is important to determine clearly which part contributes to the restriction domain and which part contributes to the nuclear scope. Concerning the question of how the tripartite structure of a *dou* sentence is formed, Hajičová, Partee and Sgall (1998) take a different perspective from that of Diesing (1992), who proposed that material in VP is mapped into the nuclear scope, whereas material external to VP is mapped into the restrictive clause. While Diesing's hypobook appears to carry significant explanatory weight in English and a number of other languages, Partee and Sgall suggest that what it actually captured is a particular grammaticalization process whose roots lie in the fact that (i) in English, German and some other languages, the subject is (to a higher or lower degree) the default topic, and (ii) there is a universal tendency for topic-focus structures to correlate with tripartite structures. In fact, this is also the way subjects and topics are related in Mandarin Chinese. Recall the mapping mechanism I postulated for the tripartite structures of different types of *dou* sentences:

(25) Left quantificational domain
    a   *dou*< phrase itself leftward (in topic) >< nuclear scope rightward (comment) >
    b   *dou*<ALT (topic focus)><the sentence minus the focus>
(26) Background quantificational domain
    c   *dou*< the rest of the sentence ><comment focus>
    d   *dou*< the rest of the sentence ><comment focus>

For the first main type of *dou* sentence, where the topic-comment partition of the construction determines the mapping to the tripartite structure, the focus-background structure does not affect the mapping, even though there is a focused element in the sentence topic (type B). Instead of determining the mapping to the tripartite structure, the topic focus introduced by *lian* provides a set of alternatives, and this set of alternatives is in turn mapped into the restriction domain.

For the second main type of *dou* sentence, where there is a focused element in the comment part of the construction, the restriction domain is provided by the entire sentence minus the focus (i.e., the background with respect to the comment focus). In this case, the background-focus structure plays a vital role in the mapping to the tripartite structure, while the topic-comment structure has nothing to do with the mapping. Compare the following two sentences, where the first one has a focused element in the topic part, and the other has a focused element in the comment part:

(27) a   [Nongcun]_Fdouyongshangkongtiao le.
         Countryside*dou*use air-conditioning le
     b   *dou*<ALT(the countryside)><have used air conditioning>
         'Even the countryside is equipped with air conditioning.'
(28) a   Nongcundouyongshang [kongtiao]_F le
         Countryside dou use air conditioning le
     b   *dou*<the country has used x><x=air conditioning>
         'The countryside has even used air conditioning.'

The focused element *nongcun* 'countryside' in the topic of the sentence, and its alternatives (such as metropolis, city and suburbs) constitutes the restrictor. This renders the predicate *having used air conditioning* under the control of the topic, whereas the focus *kongtiao* 'air conditioning' in the comment serves as the nuclear scope and is straightforwardly sensitive to the focus-sensitive operator *dou*. These two sentences illustrate that comment focus influences the mapping of the tripartite structure, whereas topic focus does not. However, in both cases, the element *dou* itself is sensitive to focus. Its sensitivity to focus shows in how it introduces different alternatives, in the case of topic focus, while determining mapping pattern, in the case of comment focus.

In this chapter, I apply the tripartite structural framework to the analysis of *dou* in Mandarin. After introducing two crucial principles of the tripartite structure – asymmetry and conservativity – I demonstrate that the quantificational tripartite analysis tool can be applied to *if*-clauses and *wulun* . . . *dou* . . . constructions. The different types of *dou* sentences map to the tripartite structure using different mechanisms. *Dou* is analyzed as a universal quantificational element; I posit that its quantificational domain may be provided by either the leftmost NP itself or the alternative set of the leftmost NP. The domain can also be provided by the background, which comprises the sentence minus the focus.

Note

1 Within Hajičová, Partee, and Sgall (1998), consult in particular the chapters on *topic-focus articulation, tripartite structures, and semantic content*.

4 Downward entailment approach

In this chapter, I will argue in detail that the Mandarin Chinese negative polarity item (NPI) *na*-CL is licensed exclusively in downward-entailing contexts; I will further show that this licensing condition can be formalized as a restriction to a universal-denoting (or 'necessity'-denoting) tripartite structure in Mandarin Chinese. The downward-entailing approach I pursue in this chapter has the additional effect of removing explanatory power for NPI distribution in Mandarin from other factors, such as episodicity and intensionality. Whether the context is episodic or not, or intensionalized or not, does not determine the distribution of non-interrogative *na*-CL noun phrases.

4.1 Critics of the non-veridicality approach

Giannakidou (1994 and following) and Zwarts (1995) propose that polarity items are excluded from veridical sentences but are allowed in non-veridical ones. Dayal (1998), too, independently proposes a similar condition on the distribution of *any*, although she does not couch this condition in terms of non-veridicality. Likewise, Lin (1996) proposes a related, though not identical, 'non-entailment-of-existence' condition for polarity phenomena in Mandarin Chinese. Lin's analysis encompasses the distribution of *renhe*, an operator analogous to *any* that appears in both free-choice and downward-entailing contexts. Curiously, however, Lin regards *renhe* as lexically ambiguous or polysemous. In addition to *renhe*, Lin's analysis captures the distribution of a set of existential polarity *wh*-phrases (EPWs), such as (*wulun*) *shei* 'no matter who, anyone' and (*wulun*) *shenme* 'no matter what, anything', which he describes as modality-sensitive items licensed 'if and only if the local proposition in which the EPW appears does not entail the existence of a referent satisfying the description of the EPW' (Lin, 1998: 246).

Horn (2000) offers some evidence against non-veridicality as the licensing condition of polarity items, arguing that it is straightforward to show that non-veridicality is neither a necessary nor a sufficient condition for licensing. His arguments proceed as follows:

Non-veridicality is not a necessary condition: Emotive factives are non-veridical but – at least when accompanied by a sense of regret or doubt – nevertheless are acceptable hosts of NPIs. See also Linebarger (1980, 1987) on why such examples are similarly problematic for Ladusaw's downward-entailment analysis:

(1) I'm [sorry/#glad] I lifted a finger to help you.

Extending this argument to Chinese, I have already demonstrated in Chapter 2, that it is similarly possible to find numerous grammatical examples of *wh*-polarity items in *dou* sentences.

Non-veridicality is not a sufficient condition: Epistemic possibility is a non-veridical operator that typically (although not always) introduces an NPI-unfriendly environment.

(2) #It's likely that anyone will win.
(3) *na-ge ren/shenme ren/renhe ren haoxiang xihuan ta。
    Which CL man/what man/any man seem like him
    Intended: 'It seems that everyone likes him.'

Haoxiang, which means 'likely' or 'possibly', suggests a non-veridical environment. Sentences containing *haoxiang* cannot license polarity items.

4.2 Downward entailment and *dou*

Since the non-veridicality approach to NPI licensing is not borne out by the facts, I will take Ladusaw's (1979) Downward Entailing Hypobook as the foundation for my analysis of Chinese polarity items in this book. We have already seen, in section 2.2 and section 4.1, that the non-veridicality approach is not sufficient to account for the full distribution of Chinese polarity items; the next task is to demonstrate that the downward-entailing approach does better in many aspects compared to the alternatives, such as the non-veridicality approach. I will take on this task in this section.

Ladusaw identifies the class of licensers for NPIs like *any* and *ever* as the class of downward-entailing functions. Kadmon and Landman propose to explain *any*'s sensitivity to these downward-entailing functions through the idea that *any* has a wider domain than other corresponding indefinites, but must make a stronger statement than those other indefinites. In order to capture the set of expressions that license NPIs, Ladusaw proposes a semantic characterization. One advantage of this semantic-driven theory is that it captures the occurrence of NPIs in the restriction of *every*, an environment that has nothing to do with negation.

Figure 4.1, cited from Ladusaw (1979), illustrates how the function of *every* is interpreted:

(4)

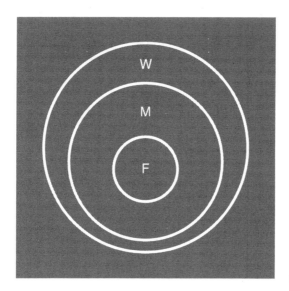

Figure 4.1

(5) F: X is a subset of Y
    $\lambda X \lambda Y \forall x[X(x) \rightarrow Y(x)]$

Ladusaw argues that the function defined in (5), when it is applied to the sets M and W, yields TRUE under Figure 4.1 (4). But if we ask whether F is monotone increasing or monotone decreasing, the answer differs depending upon which argument we consider. F will continue to yield TRUE in Figure 4.1 (4) so long as we choose to replace M with one of its subset – for example, set F. This means that the expression will be monotone decreasing with respect to its first argument. However, when we consider replacing W, F will continue to yield TRUE only if W is replaced by one of its *supersets* in Figure 4.1 (4). That is to say, F is monotone increasing with respect to its second argument position.

The expression in (6) captures the characteristics of a function that is monotone decreasing with respect to its first argument; the expression in (7) captures the characteristics of a function that is monotone increasing with respect to its second argument:

(6) $\forall X \forall Y \forall Z \Box [[X \subseteq Z \rightarrow [f(Z,Y) \rightarrow f(X,Y)]]$
(7) $\forall X \forall Y \forall Z \Box [[Y \subseteq Z \rightarrow [f(X,Y) \rightarrow]f(X,Z)]$

The previous two formulas correspond to the standard formulas for the first and second argument, respectively, of a universal operator. Therefore, the first argument slot of *every* is a legal environment for NPIs, but the second is not. See the following examples:

(8) Every student who has ever gone to China likes Chinese people.
(9) *Every student who has ever gone to China likes any Chinese people.

Although there is no perfect identical counterpart to English *every* in Mandarin, the universal operator *dou* does seem to exhibit parallel behavior with *every* in terms of the direction of entailment with respect to the operator's two argument slots:

(10) Xue yuyanxue de xuesheng dou lai canjia le juhui
 Learn linguistics de student *dou* come attend le party
 'All the students who learn linguistics came to the party.'
(11) Xue jufaxue de xuesheng *dou* lai canjia le juhui
 Learn syntax de student *dou* come attend le party
 'All the students who learn syntax came to the party.'

Sentence (10) entails sentence (11), and the noun phrase *xue yuyanxue de xuesheng* 'students who learn linguistics' in the restriction of (10) is entailed by the noun phrase *xue jufaxue de xuesheng* 'students who learn syntax' in the restriction of (11). This shows that the restriction domain of *dou* is a monotone-decreasing environment, just like the restriction domain of *every*.

Dou's nuclear scope also displays parallel behavior with that of *every*. For example, sentence (12) entails sentence (10). Whereas, in terms of the restriction domain, it is (10) that entails (36), in terms of the nuclear scope, it is the noun phrase *xili de juhui* 'party of the department' in the nuclear scope of (11) and the noun phrase *juhui* 'party' in the nuclear scope of (12) that show the same direction of entailment.

(12) Xue yuyanxue de xuesheng *dou* lai canjia le xili de juhui
 Learn linguistics de student *dou* come attend le department departy
 'All the students who learn linguistics came to the department party.'

Thus, we can see that the nuclear scope of *dou* is a monotone-increasing environment. Given the downward-entailing property in its first argument and the upward-entailing property in its second argument, we can make a prediction as follows: negative polarity items can be licensed in the restriction domain of *dou*, but not in its nuclear scope. See the following examples:

(13) Shenme xuesheng dou lai canjia le juhui
 What student *dou* come attend le party
 'All the students came to the party.'

(14) *Xuesheng dou lai canjia le shenme juhui
Students *dou* come attend le what party
Intended: 'Students came to all the parties.' Or 'Students came to some party.'

Recall that the tripartite structure introduced by *dou* is the same as the tripartite structure introduced by a standard universal operator. In cases where the topic-comment partition of the *dou* construction determines the mapping to the tripartite structure (the first type of *dou*; see previous chapter for details), *dou*'s two syntactic argument slots correspond to the restrictor and nuclear scope of its tripartite structure. That is, if the restriction domain is provided by the phrase to the left of *dou*, the mapping of the tripartite structure is parallel to the topic-comment argument sequence in linear order.

As I demonstrated extensively in Chapter 3, polarity items in Mandarin can only appear to the left side of *dou* in the first type. That is, they are licensed in the restriction domain of *dou*. I emphasize here that it is the restriction domain specifically (rather than just the left side of *dou*) that is responsible for the licensing of polarity items, because it is the goal of this book to capture the essential generalization of all NPI-licensing environments in Mandarin Chinese, rather than just listing the cases of their surface distribution.

Let us now turn to another piece of evidence which demonstrates that the first argument of *dou* is monotone decreasing when it co-occurs with polarity items. Remember that I have argued that the *wulun . . . dou . . .* construction can be divided into a series of *ruguo . . .* conditionals. That being the case, if the antecedent clause of an *if*-conditional allows entailment from its interpretation on a set to its interpretation on a subset, then there is good reason to expect that entailment proceeds in the same direction for a *wulun . . . dou . . .* sentence.

4.3 The two argument slots of *dou*

Based on the discussion in the preceding section, we can conclude that the upward-entailing nuclear scopes of the two types of *dou* exclude polarity items, as illustrated in (15) and (16).

- Left quantificational domain

    (15) *Tamen dou kanguo shenme/na-ben/renhe shu le.
    They dou read guo what/which-CL/any book le
    Intended: 'They read all books.'

- Background quantificational domain

    (16) *Ta dou xihuan chi shenme
    He all like eat what
    Intended: 'He likes eating anything.'

Even if *shenme* appears in the nuclear scope, it can only be bound by an interrogative operator, not by a polarity item. Consider the following example:

(17) Ta dou xihuan chi shenme?
 He all like eat what
 'What all does he like eating?'
(18) $\forall x$ [he likes eating x $\rightarrow$ Qy [x = y & thing(y)]]

Then, only restriction domains that bear the downward-entailing property remain as suitable candidates for hosting NPIs. But, as the data shows, only restriction domains that belong to the first type of *dou* allow *wh*-polarity items.

- Left quantificational domain

 (19) Shenme/ na-ben/ renhe shu dou kanguo le.
  What/which-CL /any book dou read guo le
  'All books have been read.'

As for the second type of *dou* construction, the polarity reading does not persist. For example, (20) cannot be interpreted to mean that everyone only writes science fiction. In other words, when there is a focus in the comment part of a sentence, *shenme* in the topic is blocked from receiving a polarity reading. Why?

- Background quantificational domain

 (20) *shenme ren dou xie de [kehuan xiaoshuo]$_F$
  What man dou write de science fiction
  Intended: 'People all wrote science fiction.'

Since the restriction domain of *dou* is the same as that of *every* with respect of monotonicity, why does it require an additional condition to license polarity items? How come the left quantificational domain of *dou* can license polarity items while the background domain cannot?

I will start my defense of the downward-entailment approach by addressing this question: why can't polarity items be licensed in the background part of the construction, even though this is a downward-entailing position? See the following contrast for example:

(21) Ta dou xie de [kehuan xiaoshuo]$_F$
 he dou write de science fiction
 'All he writes is science fiction.'
(22) *shenme ren dou xie de [kehuan xiaoshuo]$_F$
 What man dou write de science fiction
 Intended: 'All that everyone writes is science fiction.'

Downward entailment approach 73

Example (22) cannot be analyzed in the same manner as (21), where the focus item 'science fiction' falls in the comment part, as the following formula shows:

(23) $\forall x[\exists y [x = y \ \& \ person(y)]$ wrote $x \rightarrow x =$ science fiction]

Shenme in (22) can only be bound by an interrogative operator; see the interpretation as follows:

(24) shenme ren dou xie de [kehuan xiaoshuo]$_F$?
What man dou write de science fiction
'What men all write science fiction?'

This echo question is interpreted as follows:

(25) $\forall x[Qy [x = y \ \& \ person(y)]$ wrote $x \rightarrow x =$ Science Fiction]

However, if we replace *shenme ren* with *shei* 'who', (22) can be (at least marginally) interpreted to mean that all the fiction that everyone writes is science fiction. This interpretation may not be totally acceptable, but *shei* is definitely better than *shenme* in this situation. This contrast may be due to the fact that *shei* has a singular number feature. This feature reduces the chance that *shei* might associate with *dou* directly and take on a universal reading.

Alternatively, this contrast between *shei* and *shenme* might be explained by the fact that *shei* is licit with an existential operator, while *shenme* in sentence-initial position prefers a universal operator. As a result, it competes with the focus for association with *dou* and loses the fight. However, as soon as two universal operators are present in the sentence, there is no longer any competition between *shenme* in the topic and focus in the comment. See the following sentence:

(26) Shenme ren **dou zhi** xie de Ta dou xie de [kehuan xiaoshuo]$_F$
Shenme ren dou zhi xie de science fiction
'All that everyone writes is science fiction.'
(27) $\forall x[\forall y[y \in men \rightarrow y$ write $x] \rightarrow x =$ Science Fiction]

Sentence (26) has two quantificational operators, *dou* and *zhi*, both of which can be interpreted as universal quantifiers. The semantics shown in (27) suggests that the polarity items are sensitive to the downward-entailing property of the most embedded tripartite structure. In (26), *shenme* and 'science fiction' are bound by *dou* and 'only', respectively.

Although only the first type of *dou* allows *wh*-polarity items in its restriction domain, *dou* sentences with the second type of mapping mechanism can also license polarity items. In this case, the left-hand position of *dou* (which will be

74 *Downward entailment approach*

assigned to the restriction domain of a universal operator) can contain *conglai* 'ever' in Mandarin. For example:

(28) Ta conglai dou xiede [kehuan xiaoshuo]$_F$
      he ever dou write de science fiction
      'All he has ever written is science fiction.'

4.4 Three forms of *dou* sentences

With the exception of the *conglai* 'ever' sentence shown above, it is always the left quantificational domain of *dou*, rather than its background domain or its nuclear scope, that serves as a valid context for polarity items. This licensing context can be realized by three forms, as follows:

(29) Wulun   A   dou   B
      Suoyou A   dou   B
      Lian   A   dou   B

The quantificational type of *dou* illustrated here was discussed in detail in Chapter 3, which introduced the different types of *dou*. (Recall that all the *dou* sentences shown in (29) can omit their introducing element and appear as a seemingly bare *dou* sentence.)

Although all these three types of *dou* sentences exhibit the same mapping mechanism when they are analyzed using a tripartite structure, the restriction domains of the three instances of *dou* are assigned in different ways. The A segment in *wulun . . . dou . . .* and *suoyou . . . dou . . .* sentences maps straightforwardly to the restriction domain, resulting in a tripartite structure *dou*; conversely, the tripartite structure of *lian . . . dou . . .* sentences maps the alternative set of A (rather than A itself) as its restriction domain, resulting in *dou*.

There are two issues that need to be addressed here. First, one of the most frequently used polarity items in Mandarin is *renhe*. Since, on the morphological level, *renhe* already contains the concessive element *ren*, which is semantically equivalent to *wulun* 'regardless of', *wulun* must be omitted when *renhe* occurs.

Second, for *lian . . . dou . . .* sentences, the focus element that precedes *dou* introduces a set of similar alternatives. As a result, the focus itself must bear some kind of end-of-scale meaning, similar to what Horn described for polarity items. Based on the discussion in previous chapters, we can predict that all minimizer phrases, such as *yi-fen-qian* 'one cent' in Mandarin, will fit naturally into this usage. As I discussed earlier, some particular *lian . . . dou . . .* sentences with minimizers have frozen into four-syllable idioms, such as *yi-wen-bu-ming* 'having no money at all' and *hao-fa-wu-sun* 'not being hurt at all'.

4.5 Applying tripartite structure

4.5.1 The challenge from lian . . . dou . . . constructions

A new challenge for the downward-entailing approach arises from *lian . . . dou . . .* sentences: the position between *lian* and *dou* is not a downward-entailing context – at least, not at first blush. Consider the inference from (30) to (31) below:

(30) Ta lian hongsede da fangzi dou mai le
he lian red big house dou buy le
'He even bought a red big house.'
(31) Ta lian hongsede fangzi dou mai le
He lian red house dou buy le
'He even bought a red house.'

The relationship between these two sentences shows that the position between *dou* and *lian* is an upward-entailing context. That is, if he has bought a red big house, it must be true that he has bought a red house. Yet, we have also seen that this position is compatible with polarity minimizers. For example,

(32) Ta lian yidi shui dou liugei le haizi
He lian one drop water dou leave children
'He even left one drop of water to his children.'

Yidi shui 'one drop of water' is a minimizer like English 'a finger' in 'lift a finger'. Here is a situation where a UE environment licenses a polarity item. Does it therefore present a counterexample against the downward-entailing approach? I suggest that it does not. Rather, I contend that this is actually one of the main pieces of evidence that supports an application of the tripartite structure to defend the downward-entailing approach. Specifically: I propose that the inference here is assessed at the level of the tripartite structure, rather than the surface level. The restriction domain of *dou* in this situation still constitutes a downward-entailing context since buying an element from the alternate set of (red houses) entails buying an element from the alternate set of (big red houses).

4.5.2 Von Fintel's (1999) remedy vs. tripartite structure's remedy

Specifying the level at which downward entailment should be assessed can solve another problem for the downward-entailing approach. This problem can be illustrated by the following English sentence containing the polarity item *any*:

(33) 'Only John ate any vegetables for breakfast.'

This sentence is grammatical, but the position where *any* appears does not appear to be a downward-entailing context, since it does not allow inference from general to specific. See the illustration below:

(34) a   Kale → vegetable
     b   Only John ate vegetables for breakfast.
         ≠→ Only John ate kale for breakfast.

76 Downward entailment approach

A solution to this problem is proposed by von Fintel (1999). He suggests that, when we assess entailment, we must take for granted the presuppositions of the conclusion. So in this case, the presupposition (35) must be incorporated into the process of deriving entailment. Once this presupposition is taken into account, the inference goes smoothly, as follows:

(35) a Kale → vegetable
     b Only John ate vegetables for breakfast.
     c John ate kale for breakfast.
    → Only John ate kale for breakfast.

Actually, Beaver and Clark (2003, pp. 330–331) have found many examples where only/ever co-occur with minimizers such as 'give a damn' and 'lift a finger':

(36) We only ever had cream of mushroom.
(37) The central problem is that it is only ever possible to sample a child's language over a fixed period of time and within a finite number of situations.
(38) Well, I certainly don't give a damn. I only gave a damn because I thought you did.
(39) They're vicious, greedy buggers who'd only lift a finger to save their best friend if they thought they'd profit from it.

This situation is not only found in English. Using web searches, Beaver and Clark (2008, pp. 187–188) located several naturally occurring examples of equivalents of *only* in Dutch, Spanish and German licensing NPIs.

(40) Jan heeft ooit alleen maar geld aan zijn [moeder]F gegeven. (Dutch)
      'Jan only ever gave money to his [mother]F.'
(41) Hans hat nur in dem [haus]F einen Muckser von sich gegeben. (German)
      'Hans only made so much as a peep in the [house]F.'
(42) Solamente una lampara dijo una palabra y me condujo a salva hasta la habitacion (Spanish)
      'Only a lamp said a word and led me in safety up to our quarters.'

Besides these data, similar phenomenon can also been found in Mandarin. In the following sentence, the exclusive operator *zhi* 'only' can license *conglai* 'ever' which has been argued as a polarity item in the literature.

(43) Ta conglai zhi xie kehuan xiaoshuo
      He ever only writes science fiction
      'All he writes is science fiction.'

However, *zhi* does not support an inference from a more general information to a more specific information. There is no entailment relationship between the first sentence a) to the second b):

(44) a Ta conglai zhi xie xiaoshuo
       He ever only writes fiction
       'All he writes is fiction.'

(45) b Ta conglai zhi xie kehuan xiaoshuo
       He ever only writes science fiction
       'All he writes is science fiction.'

Therefore, this is a universal problem for a traditional DE approach since there are some exclusive focus-sensitive operators that are not DE which can co-occur with polarity items. We will argue that this question can also be solved within the downward-entailing approach without appealing to underlying presuppositions – by applying a tripartite structure. That is, the sentence could be analyzed with a tripartite structure as follows, where the position licensing *any* is in the downward-entailing restriction domain of a universal operator.

(46) $\forall x[x$ ate vegetable for breakfast $\rightarrow x =$ John$]$

Using this solution, we can resolve the problem without deviating from the downward-entailing approach – and at the same time, we can present a much simpler and tidier analysis than von Fintel does.

4.5.3 When von Fintel's remedy fails

Appealing to a tripartite structure is also more attractive in the next case, where von Fintel's argument fails. Consider the following sentence:

(47) Ni zaofan yiding chi le shuiguo
      You breakfast must eat le fruit
      'You must eat some fruit for breakfast.'

Under von Fintel's remedy, in order to guarantee downward entailment at the surface level, we would have to posit that this sentence presupposes that you have already eaten fruit for breakfast. Obviously, however, this is inappropriate; this failure of von Fintel's remedy presents a good illustration that not every sentence has an appropriate presupposition. That is, the additional condition (48) cannot be always added to the process for calculating the inference.

(48) a apple $\rightarrow$ fruit
     b you must eat some fruit for breakfast
     c you ate an apple for breakfast
     $\rightarrow$ You must eat an apple for breakfast.

Yet, despite the failure of von Fintel's remedy, the object position here can hold a polarity item, *shenme*:

(49) Ni zaofan yiding chi le shenme
      You breakfast must eat le what
      'You must eat something for breakfast.'

Fortunately, this problem can be solved within the downward-entailing approach by applying a tripartite structure. I argue a speculative sentence like (50) is not a complete construction; in its full form, it should be followed by an overt or covert consequent clause presenting the reasoning behind the speculation, as in (51):

(50) Ni zaofan yiding chi le shenme
You breakfast must eat le what
'You must eat something for breakfast.'
(51) Ni zaofan yiding chi le shenme cai bu shufu de
You breakfast must eat le what only not comfortable de
'You do not feel well only because you ate something special for breakfast.'

The consequent clause is necessary because the polarity items here are coupled with some particular quality that, from the point of view of the speaker, requires a certain result to be brought about.

Mandarin often uses the indefinite classifiers *ge* and *dianr* to mark the particular quality of a polarity item. For example,

(52) Wo xiawu mai le *(dianr) shenme
I afternoon buy le dianr shenme
'I bought something special this afternoon.'

In this episodic sentence, *shemme* cannot appear without *dianr*. This is a serious problem for the non-veridicality approach, for which proponents of that approach have not yet provided a convincing solution.

However, the distribution of these polarity items, and their association with a particular quality, receives a consistent account under the downward-entailing approach. Sentence (52) can be mapped to an antecedent *zhiyou-cai* construction that denotes a necessary condition like (53).

(53) Wo xiawu mai le *(dianr) shenme cai hui huilai zheme wan de.
I afternoon buy le dianr what only will back so late de
'I came back so late because I spent time buying something.'

All *zhiyou* P *cai* Q constructions can be analyzed using the following logical semantics:

(54) zhiyou P cai Q = if not P, then not Q. = Q or not P = for every s, s is not Q, then s is not P.

Based on these semantics, we can see that 'not P' turns out to be the nuclear scope of a universal operator. It's upward entailing. So, conversely, P itself is *downward* entailing. That's why polarity items can appear in P.

It has been argued that non-interrogative *shenme* also has an unusual reading not related to polarity. For example, it is possible for *ta mei chi shenme* to mean 'he ate something, but it is not worth mentioning, or it is not significant'. But I suspect that this meaning is just a presupposition or an inference of *ta mei chi shenme*; the proper meaning of this sentence is 'he did not eat any particular thing', where *shenme* is just a polarity item with a particular quality.

4.6 *If*-conditionals, tripartite structure and downward entailment

Aside from the merits discussed above, there is one more advantage gained by applying tripartite structures to polarity theory: it allows us to capture a generalization common to other unexpected contexts that turn out to be valid for polarity items. According to Stalnaker (1978) and others, bare conditionals (without any modal or quantifier) can carry the function of restricting a covert necessity operator that introduces the tripartite structure of a universal quantifier.

Recall the three situations in which a Mandarin *na*-CL construction can occur in a non-interrogative use:

(55) ① Protasis of a conditional
② A pre-*dou* position
③ A negative sentence with *ye*

Among these three environments, negation behaves the most typically: a *na*-CL construction in a negative sentence with *ye* licenses an inference from a superset to a subset with respect to its two argument slots. As to *dou*, I have shown that the restriction domain in this case is a downward-entailing context. However, before we can draw the conclusion that *na*-CL polarity items in Mandarin can be licensed by downward entailment, we'll need to check what happens in the protasis of conditionals in Mandarin as well – that is, in *ruguo* . . . clauses. We know that the other two environments are downward entailing; what's the monotonicity of the third one?

Although there are few studies on the monotone-increasing (or decreasing) property of *ruguo* . . . clauses in Mandarin, research on their English counterpart-*if*. . . clauses may provide helpful insight. After all, *if*. . . clauses are well studied, and are widely known as a very typical environment for licensing polarity items.

Let's consider what happens in *if* . . . *then* . . . sentences first. *If* . . . *then* . . . sentences in English can be interpreted as carrying a material implication in the Fregean tradition. According to this tradition, *if* . . . *then* . . . is simply a truth-functional connective, and as such is unlikely to share any responsibility in the universal force of the sentence. According to Stalnaker, Lewis and Kratzer, *if*-clauses have a uniform semantic function: the function of restricting an operator. The operator may appear overtly in the form of a quantifying adverb or a modal; alternatively, it may be a covert necessity operator. The latter option gives rise to the bare conditional, which expresses conditional necessity. (It happens to be the case that there is no null possibility operator in English; as a result, a bare conditional cannot express conditional possibility). Later in this study, I will explore in more detail the difference between necessity and universal quantification. For the moment, let us put it aside and consider the following Chinese *ruguo*-conditional:

(56) Ruguo shi ben hao shu, wo jiu xihuan
 If be CL good book I will like
 'If it is a good book, I will like it.'
(57) If [good book (x)] [I like x] (tripartite structure)
(58) ∀x [good book (x)→I like x] (material implication)

The material implication expressed by (56) is also the interpretation of the following sentence:

(59) Haoshu wo dou xihuan
 Good book I *dou* like
 'I like all the good books.'
(60) Dou [good books][I like]

The *ruguo*-conditional looks very similar to a universal expression from the perspective of its tripartite structure. In fact, I propose it *is* in fact a universal, and that a tripartite structure can thus be applied to analyze *if . . . then . . .* sentences. Under this analysis, the operator assigned to the tripartite structure of an *if . . . then . . .* sentence is a universal operator, just like the one assigned to a universal sentence. Returning to the situation in Mandarin Chinese, this will mean that the tripartite structures of *dou* sentences and *ruguo . . .* sentences share the same universal operator when performing a mapping operation.

A question arises from this analysis: why can a single tripartite structure be applied to both *dou* sentences and *ruguo . . .* sentences in the same time? The answer has to do with the linguistic status of tripartite structures. What is crucial to remember here is that two sentences having the same tripartite structure does not mean they will have the same semantic meaning. Tripartite structures indicate certain properties of the semantic interpretation of a sentence, but they do not express the semantic meaning itself, and they are not representations of a particular linguistic level in a grammar. That is, tripartite structures do not necessarily represent *the* linguistic structure of an utterance, although they do represent some properties that different linguistic structures may have in common (cf. Hajičová, Partee and Sgall, 1998).

For our purposes, the most important generalization about *ruguo . . .* and *dou* sentences captured by the tripartite structure is the monotonicity of these sentences with respect to their two arguments. That is: the first argument of a tripartite structure introduced by a universal operator is monotone decreasing, whereas its second argument is monotone increasing. Earlier, I introduced Ladusaw's proof to demonstrate the monotonicity of the two argument slots of *every*. The same reasoning process also applies to other universal quantifiers serving as operators for tripartite structures as well.

4.7 The difference between *dou*-conditionals and *ruguo*-conditionals

Now that we have seen how *ruguo*-conditionals and *dou* sentences in Mandarin can be unified – by appealing to a tripartite structure analysis and downward entailment – let's consider what distinguishes these two types of sentences from each other. Consider the following two examples, which are identical except for the elements introducing their respective antecedent clauses:

- *Ruguo* – Conditional

    (61) Ruguo na-ge huaidan qifu ni, ni jiulai zhao wo
    If which-CL bastard bully you you then come find me
    'If there is a bad person bullying you, you come to me.'

- *Dou* – Conditional

    (62) Wulun na-ge huaidan qifu ni, ni dou lai zhao wo
    No-matter which-CL bastard bully you you *dou* come find me
    'No matter which bad person is bullying you, you come to me.'

The *dou* sentence in (62) requires that there exists at least one bad person bullying you; the *ruguo* ... sentence in (61), on the other hand, does not entail the existence of any bullying event at all. This simple example illustrates that the restriction domain of *dou* has a cardinality requirement that the restriction domain of *ruguo* lacks: it must contain more than one member, and it cannot be empty.

To put this in another way, the pre-*dou* position is a restrictive quantificational position which disallows empty sets. Consider the following truth table for *ruguo* ... conditionals and *dou* sentences, respectively, (Table 4.2):

(63)

Table 4.2

	Ruguo P name Q	
P	Q	P→Q
1	1	1
0	1	1
1	0	0
0	0	1

	P dou Q	
P	Q	P *dou* Q
1	1	1
0	1	Neither 1 or 0
1	0	0
0	0	Neither 1 or 0

82   *Downward entailment approach*

The truth table for *dou* shows that grammatical *dou* sentences disallow the denotation of the pre-*dou* expression to be empty.

So far, in this chapter, I have demonstrated a unifying thread among the three environments that license polarity items: I have shown that all three environments have a downward-entailing monotonicity, and that this characteristic is what makes these environments valid licensors of polarity items. A new question arises from this analysis: given that negation is the prototypical downward-entailing context, why are negative environments alone not able to license *na*-CL without the help of *dou* or *ye*? I turn to this question next, within the scope of a larger discussion about the difference between *shenme* and *na*-CL constructions.

4.8 Another challenge for the downward-entailing approach

Now, consider the following situation: in a standard negation, both two argument slots are downward entailing, there is no intersection between X and Y and neither set has subsets that intersect with the other (Figure 4.2). Why, then, can't polarity items be licensed in the first argument, X?

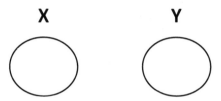

Figure 4.2

(64)   no [X] [Y], no (↓, ↓)

- *The second argument slot of the negative marker can host an NPI:*

(65)   Wo meiyou canjia shenme/na-chang/renhe bisai
        I not attend what/which-CL/any competition
        'I did not attend any competition.'

- *But the first argument slot of the negative marker cannot host an NPI:*

(66)   * shenme ren/*na-chang ren/*renhe ren meiyou canjia bisai
        What man/which-CL man/any man not attend competition
        Intended: 'Nobody attended the competition.'

I suggest that, when a polarity item appears in the first argument slot of a negative sentence, the Q operator will bind that NPI unless a *dou* or *ye* is present.

If a *dou* or *ye* is added after the polarity item, as in (66), the sentence can be rescued. Observe the result:

(67) shenme ren/na-chang ren/renhe ren dou/ye meiyou canjia bisai
What man/which-CL man/any man dou/ye not attend competition
'Nobody attended the competition.'

We've already thoroughly explored the functions of *dou* in the previous chapters, but the behavior of *ye* deserves further discussion here. I propose that, like *even*, *ye* is a focus-sensitive operator whose function is to pick out the least likely individual from the given set of alternatives. When accompanying a polarity item, it must occur in a downward-entailing environment in order to satisfy this function. See the following example:

(68) Shenme/ na-bu/renhe dianying ye buneng chaoyue Gone with the wind.
What/which-CL/any movie ye not can override Gone with the wind
'There is no movie better than *Gone with the Wind*.'

Ye displays a very similar pattern of behavior as the particle *even*, and we have already seen in previous chapters that *even* is regarded as part of the lexical meaning of polarity items by many researchers (e.g., Lee and Horn, 1994; Krifka, 1995; Lahiri, 1998). According to these authors, a phrase with *even* picks out the least likely individual from the given set of alternatives. Likelihood here is understood as a possibility scale in the sense of Horn (1972, 1989). To put it in formal semantic terms, I can draw an inference of likelihood from (68) as follows:

(69) likelihood (a common movie overrides *Gone with the Wind* for me)
→ likelihood (a good movie overrides *Gone with the Wind* for me)

In summary, with the help of the particle *ye*, the domain-widening function of *na*-CL constructions in a negation context (∈ downward entailment) yields a stronger statement, which satisfies the licensing requirement of polarity items according to the downward-entailing approach (Kadmon and Landman, 1993 and others). It thus seems reasonable to posit that the focus-sensitive operator of negative polarity – which is realized morphologically in some languages, like Hindi (Lahiri, 1998), and realized covertly in some other languages, like English (Krifka, 1995) – is syntactically realized for *na*-CL constructions in Mandarin by the particle *ye*. Note that *na*-CL in such cases is only allowed in the pre-*ye* position.

After reviewing the critique of the non-veridicality approach presented in Chapter 2, this chapter focuses in on the alternative: the traditional downward-entailing approach. I pay particular attention to ways in which this approach is well suited and less well suited to Chinese *dou* sentences. I describe the different mapping mechanisms available to *dou*'s tripartite structure and argue that polarity items can be licensed in the downward-entailing position of *dou*'s quantificational domain. This configuration is sufficient to describe both left-quantification and background quantification with *dou*. I show that the Chinese negative polarity item *na*-CL is licensed exclusively in downward-entailing contexts, and demonstrate how this licensing condition can be formalized as a restriction to a necessity-denoting tripartite structure in Mandarin Chinese.

5 *Dou* as a necessity operator

So far in this book, I have talked a lot about the quantificational properties of *dou*, including its tripartite structure, its universal quantificational power and the cardinality requirement of its first argument. All these properties play a role in determining how *dou* functions to license polarity items. In this chapter, I will build on this basic understanding of *dou* by examining its properties and behavior with respect to modality. This will also help shed light on *dou*'s licensing of polarity items.

At first blush, it may seem that modality has few connections with quantification. In fact, however, the two concepts do share some fundamental properties, from both the theoretical and empirical perspectives. According to Heim (1982), the modal relation that an operator expresses is its 'quantificational force' – necessity, possibility, etc. A modal operator is a product of three different parameters: a modal relation, a modal base and an ordering source. A modal relation is the logical operation the operator performs (be it necessity, possibility or another similar concept); a modal base defines an accessibility relation on the set of possible worlds. Thus, for example, 'w R_B w''' is to be read: w is accessible from w'. An ordering source defines a relation of relative closeness to an ideal on the set of possible worlds. Given an ordering source O, then, 'w $\leq$ o w''' is read: w is at least as close as to the ideal as w'.

Among the three parameters that jointly determine the interpretation of a modal utterance, the modal base parameter tends to be a lexical property of the modal operator itself, while the other two parameters – the modal base and the ordering source – are generally supplied by the context of the utterance.

5.1 Human necessity vs. universal quantification

The word 'must' expresses the modal relation of so-called 'human necessity'. Heim (1982) presents a comparison between necessary and universal quantification, again building on Kratzer's work. Simplifying Kratzer's definition slightly:

(1) P is a human necessity in w with respect to R_B and $\leq$ o iff p is true in every world w' which satisfies A and B:
    A: w' R_B w
    B: for every w'' R_B w: w' $\leq$ o w''

Based on this definition, we can see that human necessity is weaker in two respects than universal quantification over the entire set of possible worlds. First, it is weaker because it ranges only over accessible worlds (this is the 'A' part of the equation above); second, it is weaker because, even among the accessible worlds, it ranges only over those that are closest to the ideal (this is the 'B' part of the equation). To better understand the definition of human necessity, consider Kratzer's analysis for an example like (2):

(2) Felix must be taken to the vet.

If we adopt the definition of human necessity above, the analysis of this sentence will proceed as Kratzer said: 'In the interpretation of (2) (under a natural reading), the modal relation of human necessity combines with certain contextually furnished choices for the modal base and the source. A likely ordering source would be one which ranks worlds in terms of their closeness to an ideal of proper care for a pet. 'w ≤ o w'' thus amounts to: in w, pets are cared for at least as properly as in w'. The modal base would plausibly be one which excludes from accessibility those worlds in which Felix is already dead, or in which certain other facts obtain that would make taking him to the vet impossible or pointless.

Given these choices, (2) is predicted to be true if Felix is taken to the vet in all worlds that are accessible in the sense alluded to and in which pets are cared for at least as properly as in any other accessible world.

5.2 Human necessity vs. *if* ... *then* ... sentence

In Kratzer's theory, *if* . . . clauses behave just like human necessity constructions, with one difference: the modal base that enters into the interpretation of the *if*-clause is not contributed by the context alone, but is a product of contextual factors *plus* the meaning of the *if*-clause. The function of the *if*-clause is to limit accessibility to, at most, those worlds in which the statement in that clause is true. Consider the following example of an *if*-clause cited from Heim (1982):

(3) If Felix was exposed to weed killer (a brand), he must be taken to the vet.

In Kratzer's theory, the interpretation of (3) is very similar to the interpretation of (2), with one crucial difference: the modal base that enters into the interpretation of (3) is not contributed by the context alone, but a product of contextual factors and the meaning of the *if*-clause. So if (3) is uttered in a context which is in all relevant respects like the context that we assumed above for the utterance of (2), then R_B will not just exclude worlds where Felix is already dead or otherwise unable to go to the vet, but will also exclude any worlds in which Felix was not exposed to weed killer. In other words, a necessity condition for 'w' R_B w' to obtain will be that Felix was exposed to weed killer in w'. The ordering source will be as before, and 'must' again expresses human necessity. Consequently, the predicted truth condition for (3) is this: (3) is true iff Felix is taken to the vet in every world w such that (i) Felix was exposed to weed killer in w and w also meets the contextually determined requirements for accessibility, and (ii) w is as close as any accessible world to the ideal of proper care for pets.

5.3 Material implication (*if*... *then*... sentences) vs. invisible-operator analysis

According to Fregean tradition, *if*... *then*... clauses bear a material implication – a truth-functional connective – and as such, do not share any responsibility in the universal force of the sentence. However, Kratzer and Heim attribute a uniform semantic function to *if*-clauses wherever they occur: the function of restricting an operator. Recall from the last chapter that this operator may be lexically overt (surfacing in the form of a quantifying adverb or a modal) or it may be syntactically covert (an unrealized necessity operator). In the latter case, we derive a bare conditional-expressing conditional necessity. Since it happens that there is no syntactically null *possibility* operator, conditional possibility cannot be expressed by a bare conditional.

According to Heim, both the modal base and ordering source used to evaluate an unrealized necessity operator are 'realistic'. A realistic modal base, in Heim's terms, specifies a reflexive accessibility relation: that is, the worlds it makes accessible from the actual world are those worlds in which certain actual facts are true. A 'realistic' ordering source, similarly, orders worlds in terms of how closely they correspond to certain actual facts. Because of these idiosyncratic limits, a covert necessity operator cannot always be replaced by an overt necessity operator without causing a change in meaning. Heim's postulation that the covert necessity operator accepts only realistic modal bases and ordering sources leads to the further hypobook that every bare conditional entails universal quantification in the actual world.

Not everybody, however, accepts Heim's analysis of bare conditionals. Cheng and Huang (1996), for example, interpret these constructions differently. Recall that, for Kratzer and Heim, bare conditionals necessarily denote *if*-clauses that restrict a syntactically unrealized necessity operator, unlike conditionals with overt operators (which may surface in the form of, for instance, a quantifying adverb or a modal). In the following English examples, (4) is a bare conditional, whereas (5) is not.

(4) If a man owns a donkey, he beats it.
(5) If a man can own a donkey, he beats it.

Cheng and Huang take a different view of bare conditionals, working from the perspective of Mandarin Chinese. For them, 'bare conditionals' are conditionals that do not have an overt quantifier such as *ruguo* 'if' in the antecedent clause, or an overt quantifier such as *dou* 'all' in the consequent clause. In this type of conditional, the word *jiu* 'then' is optionally present in the consequent clause, as we can see in the following:

(6) Shei xian lai, shei xian chi
   Who first come who first eat
   'If X comes first, X eats first.'

(7) Shei xian lai, shei jiu xian chi
    Who first come who then first eat
    'If X comes first, then X eats first.'

We can see in (7) that the presence or absence of *jiu* 'then' does not create any difference in interpretation. It's also important to note that *ruguo* can similarly be inserted at the beginning of an antecedent clause:

(8) Ruguo shei xian lai, shei jiu xian chi
    Who first come who then first eat
    'If X comes first, then X eats first.'

These *ruguo* ... *jiu* ... sentences in Mandarin behave just like *if* ... *then* ... sentences in English. So even though they approach them somewhat differently, the Mandarin bare conditionals discussed by Cheng and Huang are equivalent to the English bare conditionals discussed by Kratzer and Heim.

Based on this parallel, it seems we need to update our analysis of Mandarin *ruguo* ... *name* ... sentences without a modal (such as *keneng* 'may', *yinggai* 'should', or *bixu* 'must'); rather than understanding them as material implications, we can now interpret them as constructions performing the function of restricting an empty necessity operator.

Heim has argued that the main strength of the invisible-operator analysis of bare conditionals, compared to the rival material implication analysis, lies in the fact that it permits a uniform account of the semantic function of *if*-clauses. Those who maintain that bare conditionals express material implication must find an alternative explanation for some *if* ... *then* ... sentences, since it is clear that not all of these sentences can bear a material implication interpretation. For instance, when the *if*-clause modifies a possibility operator or one of a variety of non-universal adverbs of quantification, a material implication analysis will not work. In addition to this theoretical argument in favor of the invisible-operator analysis, there also exist arguments that are more directly based on intuitions about the meaning of bare conditionals. It has often been observed, for instance, that the mere falseness of the antecedent does not seem sufficient to render a conditional 'true', even though this conclusion should follow from first-order logic. Furthermore, conditionals that lack any kind of salient connection between the meaning of the antecedent and the meaning of the consequent often sound strange. These observations provide further evidence in favor of a theory that treats conditionals as inherently modalized, rather than as functions expressing material implication.

5.4 An updated analysis of *dou* as a conditional necessity operator

The above theoretical discussion is a necessary preamble to a deeper exploration of the real function and meaning of *dou* in Chinese. Since no exact counterpart of *dou* exists in English, the connection to *if* ... sentences here is necessarily approximate.

As I have argued in previous sections, the *wulun ... dou ...* construction is derived from a group of *ruguo ... name (jiu)* sentences of the same type. It should be noted that these *ruguo ...* sentences are bare conditionals, in the sense that they contain no other modals except a syntactically empty necessity operator. Since I have proven that bare conditional *ruguo ... name (jiu) ...* sentences, just like their English counterparts, are functions restricting an empty necessity operator, it is now possible for me to propose that *wulun ... dou ...* sentences also express conditional necessity – and further, that this conditional necessity is inherently modalized and can only be evaluated with respect to a realistic modal base and a realistic ordering source. Thus, there is a natural inference that *dou* is not just a universal operator, but a conditional necessity operator. As I have mentioned, a realistic modal base specifies a reflexive accessibility relation: worlds accessible from the actual world are those in which certain actual facts are true. A realistic ordering source is one that orders worlds in terms of how closely they correspond to certain actual facts.

Given these assumptions, it follows that the conditional necessity characteristics of *dou* sentences are inherently modalized and can only be evaluated with respect to a realistic modal base and a realistic ordering source. This hypobook gives us a new perspective from which to observe the behavior of *dou*: the perspective of modality. It follows from my proposal that every *dou* conditional entails universal quantification in the actual world. This essential property of *dou* sentences disallows the possibility that the denotation of the domain restriction of *dou* can be empty. Ultimately, we get the same result as we did above: sentences in the form 'P *dou* Q' can never be evaluated so long as P has an empty denotation.

I argued in the chapter on *dou* that *wh*-polarity items can be licensed in the restriction domain of *dou*. Since we now understand *dou* to be a conditional necessity operator rather than a universal operator, it becomes necessary to update the licensing condition for non-interrogative *wh*-elements in Mandarin from the restriction domain of an universal operator to the restriction domain of a conditional necessity operator. In fact, as it turns out, the argument for adopting this approach becomes even firmer when we take bare conditional sentences into consideration. Consider the following examples, in which *wh*-elements appear in the object and subject position of a *ruguo ...* clause, respectively:

(9) Ruguo you shenme kunnan, name women jiu xiangfangshefa zhansheng zhexie kunnan
If have what difficulty then we then try by hook or by crook overcome these difficulty
'If there are some difficulties, we will try to overcome them by hook or by crook.'

(10) Ruguo na-ge kunnan cengjing dabai guo ni, ni xia-ci jiuyao gewai xiaoxin
If which-CL difficulty ever beat guo you you next time then want extraordinarily be careful
'If you have been beaten by some difficulty, you should be extraordinarily careful of it next time.'

The two conditionals above have no modals in their antecedent clauses, so they are typical bare conditionals in Mandarin. The examples clearly illustrate that the antecedent clause of a *ruguo* . . . sentence is a valid environment for *shenme* and *na*-CL to occur as polarity items.

Recall from the previous section that conditional necessity on Kratzer's theory is just like human necessity, with one difference: the modal base that enters into the interpretation of conditional necessity is not established on the basis of context alone; instead, it is a product of contextual factors and the meaning of the *if*-clause. To compare these two situations in Mandarin Chinese, consider the following two sentences, which express conditional necessity and human necessity, respectively:

(11) Ruguo bingren tiwen dadao 39-du, jiuyao dai ta qu yiyuan
If patient body temperature reach 39 centigrade, then take him go hospital
'The patient needs to be taken to the hospital if his temperature reaches 39 degrees centigrade.'

(12) Bingren bixu qu yiyuan
Patient must go hospital
'The patient must go to the hospital.'

Next, we will use Heim and Kratzer's definitions of human necessity and conditional necessity to analyze these two sentences with subtly different meanings. In the interpretation of sentence (12) (under a natural reading), the modal relation of human necessity combines with certain contextually furnished choices for the modal base and the ordering source. A likely ordering source would be one that ranks worlds in terms of their closeness to an ideal of proper care for patients. 'w ≤ o w'' thus amounts to: in w, patients are cared for at least as properly as in w'. The modal base would plausibly be one that excludes from accessibility those worlds in which patients are already dead or in which certain other facts are true that would make taking a patient to the hospital impossible or pointless.

Given these choices, (12) is predicted to be true if patients are taken to the hospital in all worlds that are accessible in the sense alluded to, and in which patients are cared for at least as properly as in any other accessible world.

However, sentence (11) has a slightly different interpretation. Specifically, it is just like (12), with one difference: the modal base that enters into its interpretation is not contributed by the context alone, but is a product of contextual factors and the meaning of the antecedent *ruguo*-clause. The function of the *ruguo*-clause, like the function of an English *if*-clause, is to limit accessibility to, at most, those worlds in which the statement contained in that clause is true.

So, (12) is uttered in a context in which R_B excludes any world in which patients are already dead (or cannot realistically go to the hospital for some other reason), whereas (11) is uttered in a context which is in all relevant respects like the context of (12), but which furthermore excludes any worlds in which the body temperature of the patient in question has not reached 39 degrees centigrade yet.

In other words, for the necessity condition 'w' R_B w' to be met under the situation of sentence (11), the body temperature of the patient in question must have already reached 39 degrees centigrade in w'. The ordering source for (11) is as in (12). Consequently, the predicted truth condition for (11) is this: sentence (11) is true iff the patient in question is taken to the hospital in every world w such that (i) the body temperature of the patient has already reached 39 degrees centigrade in w and w also meets the contextually determined requirements for accessibility, and (ii) w is as close as any accessible world to the ideal of proper care for patients.

This discussion on conditional sentences and *bixu* 'must' sentences may seem complicated and intricate, but it is possible to extract an essential spirit from: conditional necessity is stronger than human necessity in how its modal ordering base is defined. Take the contrast between (12) and (13), for example. Example (13) is more comparable to (12) than (11).[1] It is safe to say that sentence (12) is true if sentence (13) is true, but not vice versa.

(13) Ruguo shi ge bingren, jiuyao qu yiyuan
 If be CL patient, then go hospital
 'He needs to go to the hospital if he is a patient.'

To state the comparison between the two sentences more directly, the situation can be paraphrased as follows: if 'patients must go to hospital' is a commonly accepted fact in some world w, then 'a patient like him in w needs to go to hospital' is a natural result. However, just because 'a patient should go to hospital' is true in a world w, this does not guarantee that all patients must go to hospital in w. So (13) is stronger than (12). This conclusion may seem to run counter to our first intuition, since a 'must' sentence sounds stronger than an 'if . . . then . . .' sentence. However, that is not the right judgment from the perspective of the sentences' truth values. There exists an entailment relationship between the two necessity sentences: sentence (13), with conditional necessity, entails sentence (12), with human necessity, but not the other way round. Thus, we come to the conclusion that (13) is stronger than (12).

So far, in this section, we have shown that conditional necessity is stronger than human necessity. Now, recall the temporary conclusion I drew above, that *renhe* can be licensed by both human necessity and conditional necessity, whereas non-interrogative *shenme* and *na*-CL can only be licensed by conditional necessity. A new argument can be made by combining these two statements: the licensing condition for non-interrogative *wh*-indeterminates is stricter than the licensing condition for *renhe*. The distribution of *renhe* is therefore broader than the distribution of non-interrogative *na*-CL, *shenme* and the like. To be clear, the conclusion that *renhe* has a broader distribution than non-interrogative *wh*-indeterminates is stated on the level of theory, and should not be taken to imply that it will have a higher frequency in terms of actual use.[2]

The distribution of *renhe* is said to be broader than the distribution of *wh*-polarity items because *renhe* can appear in both the human necessity context and the conditional necessity context, whereas *wh*-polarity items can only appear in the conditional necessity context. Furthermore, *renhe* can also be licensed in object positions of negative sentences, whereas *wh*-polarity items cannot. Finally, *renhe* has a broaden pattern of distribution than *na*-CL and *shenme,* in that the former can also appear in some other modal contexts such as possibility contexts, while the latter cannot. Consider the following contrast:

(14) Women keyi zhansheng *renhe* kunnan
 We can overcome *any* difficulty
 'We can overcome *any* difficulty.'
(15) *Women keyi zhansheng *shenme* kunnan
 We can overcome what difficulty
 Intended: 'We can overcome *any* difficulty.'
(16) *Women keyi zhansheng *na*-ge kunnan
 We could overcome which-CL difficulty
 Intended: 'We can overcome *any* difficulty.'

Keyi, meaning 'can', is a possibility operator. This operator, along with some other modals (such as *yinggai* 'should' and *nenggou* 'can'), can license *renhe* in Mandarin, but cannot license non-interrogative *na*-CL and *shenme* phrases. Thus, it seems pretty clear that at least in the case of modal licensing, *renhe* has a broader distribution than non-interrogative *na*-CL and *shenme* phrases.

A note is in order here: just because possibility operators such as *keyi* and *keneng* cannot license *wh*-polarity items like *shenme* and *na*-CL does not mean that these lexical items cannot ever co-occur. Consider the following examples:

(17) Shenme kunnan dou keyi bei zhansheng
 What difficult all can bei overcome
 'Every difficulty can be overcome.'
(18) Na-xiang kunnan dou keneng bei zhansheng
 Which-CL difficulty all can bei overcome
 'Every difficulty can be overcome.'

As the examples shown, *wh*-polarity items can co-occur with possibility modals, but they are not licensed by those modals; they are licensed by *dou*, the conditional necessity operator, in its restriction domain. *Dou*'s licensing capacity is independent of the power of possibility modals.

In the next section, I will flesh out the details of the conditional necessity of *dou* through a comparison with some other operators with different modality functions.

5.5 Other universal operators in Mandarin

So far, in this chapter, I have described and illustrated in detail the difference between the necessity operator and universal operator from the perspective of modality, following the analysis of Heim. In order to apply this analysis fully to

Mandarin Chinese, we need to check not only the status of *dou* sentences but also other universal operators in Mandarin. Doing so will help us accurately characterize the full distribution of *renhe*, non-interrogative *shenme*, *shei*, and *na*-CL phrases.

Starting from the hypobook that the licensing condition for Chinese polarity items is a downward-entailing environment such as the domain restriction of a universal operator (for example, the domain restriction of *dou*), it is possible to predict that the restriction domains of other universal operators in Mandarin are also licit environments for polarity items. If this argument were on the right track, the following sentences should be acceptable. But in fact, they are not:

(19) *shenme ren/na-ge ren quan lai canjia fenghui le.
    What man/which-CL man all come attend summit le
    Intended: 'Everyone comes to the summit.'
(20) *shenme ren/na-ge ren zong lai canjia fenghui.
    What man/which-CL man usually come attend summit
    Intended: 'Everyone usually comes to the summit.'

Furthermore, the behavior of *renhe* is parallel to the behavior of non-interrogative *shenme* and *na*-CL phrases in this respect. That is, *renhe*, cannot be licensed by the universal operators *quan* and *zong*. Consider the following two examples with *renhe*:

(21) *renhe konglong quan xiaoshi le
    Any dinosaur all disappear le
    Intended: 'All dinosaurs disappeared.'
(22) *renhe yilei zong shoudao paiji
    Any Heterogeneous all bear marginalized
    Intended: 'People who are different are usually marginalized.'

What, then, are the environments in which *renhe*, *shenme* and *na*-CL phrases do occur? Consider the distribution in Table 5.1. It shows the acceptability of *renhe*, *shenme* and *na*-CL phrases in a range of environments with respect to modality.

(23)

Table 5.1

	Renhe	Shenme	Na-CL
Universal operators *quan* and *zong*	*	*	*
Conditional necessity (*ruguo*-conditional)	√	√	√
Domain restriction of *dou*	√	√	√
Human necessity	√	*	*
Possibility modal	√	*	*

From this table, we can see that polarity items in Mandarin (which in this case includes items like *renhe*, non-interrogative *na*-CL and *shenme*, but not minimizers) can be divided into two groups: those containing the concessive element *ren*, and those without such an element. Based on this observation, it looks as though *renhe* constitutes a group to itself in terms of distribution, while *shenme* and *na*-CL polarity items constitute another. Interestingly, this observation also doubles as an additional piece of evidence to argue against the classification of Cheng and Giannakidou, who analyze non-interrogative *na*-CL and *renhe* as clustering together in one group and *shenme* as an element on its own.

Next, let's come back to the question of why *quan* and *zong* cannot license Chinese polarity items. *Quan* means 'all', and *zong* means 'usually'; both are standard instantiations of universal quantification in Mandarin. In both cases, their restriction domains are downward entailing, just like that of their kin *dou*. Consider the following illustration:

(24) ren chusheng de shihou quan shi shanliang de
human being born de time all be kind de
'All human beings are kind when they are born.'
(25) nüren chusheng de shihou quan shi shanliang de
women born de time all be kind de
'All women are kind when they are born.'

There is an entailment relationship from sentence (24) to sentence (25). Since women are a subset of all human beings, we can conclude that the restriction domain of *quan* is a downward-entailing environment, which allows the inference from the interpretation on a set to the interpretation on its subset. This entailment relationship will also hold if *quan* here is replaced by *zong*:

(26) dui mou xie gongzuokuang lai shuo, zhoumo zong shi hen wuliao
to some CL workaholics come say weekend usually be very boring
'The weekends are usually very boring to some workaholics.'
(27) dui mou xie gongzuokuang lai shuo, zhouri zong shi hen wuliao
to some CL workaholics come say sunday usually be very boring
'Sunday is usually very boring to some workaholics.'

There is an entailment relationship from sentence (26) to sentence (27). Since Sunday is a subset of the weekend, it can be predicted from this illustration that the first argument slot of *zong* is monotone decreasing.

So *quan* and *zong*, like *dou*, can also give rise to a downward-entailing context by introducing a tripartite structure, but they cannot license Chinese polarity items as *dou* does. Based on the discussion earlier in this chapter, we now have the tools to solve this puzzle: specifically, we can tease apart the behavior of *dou* from that of *quan* and *zong* by appealing to the distinction between a necessity operator and a universal operator. As I have argued above, *dou* is not actually a universal operator, but a necessity operator, like the *ruguo* ... conditionals. It now becomes clear that what polarity items in Mandarin are truly sensitive to is the restriction of a necessity operator – not a universal operator. Since mere universal operators are not sufficient to license Chinese NPIs, *zong* and *quan* are not suitable candidates.

This analysis rests on the assumption that *quan* and *zong* are in fact universal operators, rather than necessity operators. How can we know this is a valid assumption? Recall from the beginning of this chapter that, according to Heim (1982), human necessity is weaker in two respects than universal quantification over the entire set of possible worlds. First, it is weaker because it ranges only over accessible worlds; second, it is weaker because even among the accessible worlds, it ranges only over those that are closest to the ideal. However, *quan* and *zong* carry no requirement that their modal bases and ordering sources be realistic in terms of modality. It follows from this that sentences with *quan* or *zong* entail universal quantification in the actual world, whereas sentences with *dou* cannot always guarantee universal quantification in the non-actual world. See the following two sentences:

(28) dui mou xie gongzuokuang lai shuo, zhoumo zong shi hen wuliao
 to some CL workaholics come say weekend usually be very boring
 'The weekends are usually very boring to some workaholics.'
(29) dui mou xie gongzuokuang lai shuo, zhouri zong shi hen wuliao
 to some CL workaholics come say Sunday usually be very boring
 'Sunday is usually very boring to some workaholics.'

The entailment relationship between these two sentences with *zong* shows that the restriction domain of *zong* is also a downward-entailing position.

I propose that the difference between *dou* and *quan* (or *zong*) is parallel to the difference between an indefinite determiner with a covert necessity operator and a universal determiner. Apparently, the statement 'An F is G' does not always entail 'Every F is G.' According to Heim, 'A'-generics contrast with 'every'-NPs precisely in the sense that the former allow for exceptions. Perhaps this occurs because the combination of a necessity operator '□' with a restrictive indefinite tends to invite a stereotypical, rather than a realistic, ordering source. A stereotypical ordering source ranks worlds in terms of their closeness to an ideal of 'normality' of some sort. I argue that *dou* is parallel with 'A' plus a covert necessity operator (or a bare plural plus a covert necessary operator), while *quan* is parallel with the overt universal operator 'every' with respect to its quantificational power. This proposal can account for the following contrast:

(30) Mao dou xihuan chi yu, ke wo jia de xiaomao bu tai xihuan
 Cat *dou* like eat fish but my home de little cat not very like
 'Cats likes eating fish. But mine is not very fond of fish.'
(31) *Mao quan xihuan chi yu, ke wo jia de xiaomao bu tai xihuan
 Cat all like eat fish but my home de little cat not very like
 Intended: 'All cats like eating fish. But mine is not very fond of fish.'

96 Dou *as a necessity operator*

In each of the sentences (30) and (31), the second clause tries to cancel the assertion stated by the first clause. The contrast shows that the correction proceeds smoothly in sentences with *dou*, but less smoothly in sentences with *quan*. This contrasting pair demonstrates the difference between *dou* and *quan* in theoretical terms. Essentially, because the necessity operator *dou* invites a stereotypical ordering source (which ranks worlds in terms of their closeness to an ideal of 'normality' of some sort), it can allow exceptional or marginal samples to some extent; conversely, the universal operator *quan* or *zong* invites a realistic ordering source (which ranks worlds in terms of their closeness to the actual world), and therefore cannot allow this same degree of variance.

5.6 Updating the licensing condition for Chinese polarity items

Based on the discussion in this chapter, we can update the proposed licensing condition for Chinese NPIs as follows: non-interrogative *wh*-indeterminates in Mandarin can be licensed in the restriction domain of a necessity operator, in terms of Heim's analysis of modality. More specifically, *wh*-indeterminate polarity items are licensed by a conditional necessity operator in their restriction domain. Conditional necessity is different from human necessity in that the modal base used in the interpretation of the former is not contributed by context alone, but is a product of contextual factors plus the meaning of the antecedent clause. The function of the antecedent clause in a conditional is to limit accessibility to, at most, those worlds in which the statement proposed in the antecedent clause is true.

In terms of modality, a necessity operator differs from a universal operator in the following manner: necessity requires an actual-world domain, whereas universality does not. *Dou*-conditionals and *ruguo*-conditionals are two instances of necessity operators – more specifically, conditional necessity operators. In addition, the necessity operator *dou* invites a stereotypical ordering source, which ranks worlds in terms of their closeness to an ideal of 'normality' of some sort. Because of this, it allows exceptions and marginal samples to some extent. That's what the term 'realistic ordering source' means with respect to *dou* as a conditional necessity operator.

All the environments in which non-interrogative *shenme* and *na*-CL phrases occur can license *renhe* as a polarity item. Bare conditional *ruguo* . . . clauses and *dou* . . . sentences thus can license *renhe* as well as *na*-CL and *shenme* phrases. However, the reverse does not hold true, because the distribution of *renhe* is broader than that of *wh*-polarity items. *Renhe* can be licensed by conditional necessity, human necessity or even possibility. Thus, *renhe* is not truly sensitive to types of modality except the universal operator.

As a final note to end this chapter, it's worth considering why wholly universal operators (such as *quan* and *zong*) cannot license polarity items even though their restriction domain is one of the typical downward-entailing environments. This question is similar to a question I addressed earlier in this research, concerning why negation sentences without *ye* cannot license non-interrogative *na*-CL phrases, even though negation is a representative monotone-increasing environment. Are there outside reasons that can account for *renhe*'s being excluded by the universal operators *quan* and *zong*?

Since it is clear that not all Chinese polarity items can be licensed by negation and universality in the same manner that they are licensed by other downward-entailing contexts, it seems that our existing downward-entailing approach to Chinese polarity items requires some supplemental stipulations. Specifically, it is necessary that we narrow the range of our analysis – from downward-entailing contexts *in general* to *certain* downward-entailing contexts introduced by specific operators.

Finally, I would like to suggest one other tentative answer to the question of why *zong* and quan cannot license polarity items in the same way *dou* can. It may be that *zong* and *quan* don't actually perform a quantificational operation like *dou* does, but simply partition the sentences in which they appear. I leave further exploration of this possibility to future work. According to Guo and Lee (2016), a possible analysis is that *zong* is a VP-level modifier instead of a universal quantifier. In Mandarin, there are some temporal adverbs like *zong* which should be distinguished from Q-adverbs. The interpretation of *zong* is not semantically equivalent to the Q-adverb always: *zong* does not necessarily require a matching relationship between two arguments. If *zong* cannot introduce a tripartite structure as *dou* does, it will not affect the logic form of sentences containing it. Then, there will be no DE position in LF for polarity items to survive.

In this chapter, I build on the basic understanding of *dou* established in the preceding chapters by examining the properties and behavior of this element with respect to modality. This discussion also sheds light on *dou*'s licensing of polarity items. Based on the discussion in this chapter, I update the proposed licensing condition for Chinese NPIs as follows: non-interrogative *wh*-indeterminates in Mandarin can be licensed in the restriction domain of a necessity operator, per Heim's analysis of modality. More specifically, *wh*-indeterminate polarity items are licensed by a conditional necessity operator in their restriction domain. Conditional necessity is different from human necessity in that the modal base used in the interpretation of the former is not contributed by context alone, but is a product of contextual factors plus the meaning of the antecedent clause.

Notes

1 In earlier discussions, I used sentence (11) rather than sentence (13) to compare against sentence (12) because this made it possible to elaborate the distinction between human necessity and conditional necessity more clearly and easily.
2 Unfortunately, full statistics on the use of *renhe*, *na*-CL and *shenme* cannot be provided since no sufficiently large database is available.

6 The non-uniformity of Chinese polarity items

6.1 The indeterminate status of *wh*-elements

Polarity-sensitive *wh*-elements have long been a main topic of study in the field of polarity studies, cross-linguistically. Before presenting my full analysis of Chinese *wh*-elements, let's consider once again some previous studies that touch on relevant issues.

Kratzer (2005) supports the accepted view that indeterminate phrases do not have their own quantificational force. She agrees with a conjecture proposed by Partee (1995: 567), as follows:

(1) What appears to account for the quantificational interpretation of such sentences is the existence of various 'default' or unmarked operators with interpretations such as 'universal', 'modalized universal', and 'generic', alongside other possibilities such as implicit existential quantification.

Kratzer builds on this conjecture, arguing that in all of the cases mentioned by Partee, ungrammaticality is produced when a DP finds itself in the scope of an 'incompatible' operator.

Cross-linguistic evidence that may shed light on the nature of Chinese indeterminate pronouns can be found in studies on Japanese indeterminates (Table 6.1) by Kratzer and Shimoyama (2002), among others.

(2)
Table 6.1

Dare	who	Doko	where
Nani	what	Itu	when
Dore	which(one)	Naze	why
Dono	which(Det)	Doo	how

Depending on the operator with which they appear, Japanese indeterminate phrases can take on various interpretations, including existential, universal, negative polarity, free choice and interrogative. The operators that carry quantificational force in Japanese do not have to be adjacent to the indeterminate phrases they quantify; instead, quantification often occurs at a distance. This is illustrated by (3), an example of universal quantification, and (4), a constituent question.

(3) [[Dono hon-o yonda] kodomo] -mo yoku nemutta.
 which book-ACC read child-MO well slept
 'For every book x, the child who read x slept well.'
(4) Taro-wa [[dare-ga katta] mochi]-o tabemasita ka?
 Taro-TOP who-NOM bought rice cake-ACC ate Q
 'Who is the x such that Taro ate rice cakes that x bought?'

Nishigauchi (1986, 1990) argued that the operators shown in Table 6.1 are adverbial quantifiers that can unselectively bind variables made available by indeterminate phrases and bare noun phrases, as proposed in Heim (1982). Nishigauchi's program, which attempts to give a unified interpretation to all quantificational structures with indeterminate pronouns, looks very plausible from a typological point of view.

Kratzer and Shimoyama (2002) move closer to a unified analysis by applying Hamblin semantics (Hamblin, 1973) to the analysis of Japanese indeterminate pronouns. In Hamblin semantics, indeterminate pronouns introduce alternatives that keep expanding until they find an operator that selects them. The semantic behavior of indeterminate pronouns crucially depends on their location with respect to operators linked to existential closure, negation, universality, genericity and interrogative force, just as in unselective binding approaches. Hamblin's major innovation was a semantics based on alternatives. In more recent years, this tool has resurfaced in Mats Rooth's semantics of focus.

6.2 Application to Mandarin Chinese

In developing Hamblin semantics for Japanese indeterminate pronouns, Kratzer and Shimoyama introduce a set of alternatives. They posit that the number of alternatives keeps growing until they encounter an operator that selects alternatives. Given the high degree of similarity between Chinese indeterminate pronouns and their counterparts in Japanese, it seems plausible that this kind of Hamblin semantics can also be applied to Chinese indeterminate pronouns. The alternatives, on Kratzer and Shimoyama's analysis, can be of different semantics types, and the quantifiers can operate on alternatives of different types as well. If the alternatives are individuals, for instance, the relevant quantifiers will be the usual generalized quantifiers. Conversely, propositional alternatives will eventually be quantified by propositional operators.

Now let me illustrate the interpretation of a simple Chinese sentence like *na-ge xuesheng dou tongguo le* 'every student has passed'. For all possible worlds w and variable assignments g, we have:

(5) $[[\text{na-ge xuesheng}]]^{w,g} = \{x: \text{student}(x)(w)\}$
 $[[\text{tongguo}]]^{w,g} = \{\lambda x \lambda w'.\text{passed}(x)(w')\}$

[[na-ge *xuesheng dou* tongguo le]]^{w,g}
= {p: $\exists$x[student (x)&p = λw'.passed(x)(w')]}

Na-ge xuesheng ('which student') denotes the set of students in the evaluation world. The denotation of the verb *tongguo* ('passed') is a singleton set containing the property 'pass', which is construed as a schönfinkeled relation between individuals and worlds. The sentence *na-ge xuesheng dou tongguo le* denotes a set of propositions of the form {'Zhangsan passed', 'Lisi passed', 'Wangwu passed', etc.}.

The example above illustrates how the alternative set introduced by the indeterminate pronoun *na-ge xuesheng* grows into a set of propositional alternatives via functional application at the stage where the denotations of subject and VP combine.

Expanding Hamblin alternatives can bridge the distance between indefinites and their operators. Adopting a semantics based on alternatives allows us to establish an immediate connection to the accounts of negative polarity items and free-choice items (Krifka, 1995; Lee and Horn, 1994; Horn, 1999; Lahiri, 1998). Krifka (1995) develops his consideration of English *any* within an alternative semantics where negative polarity items introduce individual alternatives that can be ordered with the item itself. According to Krifka, polarity items are just a special case of other constructions that introduce alternatives, like expressions in focus and expressions that are part of a linguistic scale and introduce scalar implicatures (Krifka, 1995).

I propose that applying Hamblin semantics to *wh*-polarity items in Mandarin will allow us to define the correct syntactic relationship between the polarity items and their operators. This relationship is not subject to c-command or linear precedence, as previous studies have claimed. Based on the data and investigation I have accumulated, I argue that a *wh*-polarity item and its binding operator are Hamblin-semantically related. That is, they belong to the same syntactic structure and are nearest to each other within this structure. A *wh*-polarity item can be located to the left or right of its licensing operator as long as they are closest to each other within their syntactic structure and as embedded as possible.

6.3 Morphological variations of *wh*-elements

In contrast to Indo-European indefinites, which tend to be built from a common core plus additional material, Japanese and Chinese indeterminate pronouns are morphologically simple. It therefore seems reasonable that the differences between Japanese and Chinese indeterminate pronouns, on the one hand, and Indo-European indefinites, on the other, should derive from that visible morphological distinction.

As part of his survey of indefinite pronouns and determiners, Haspelmath (1997) discusses Latvian *wh*-elements and their morphological variations. See Table 6.2, cited from his work, which illustrates the indeterminate pronouns in Latvian:

(6)

Table 6.2

	Interrogative	kaut-series	ne-series	jeb-series
person	Kas	kaut kas	ne-viens	jeb-kads
thing	kas	kaut kas	ne-kas	jeb-kas
place	kur	kaut kur	ne-kur	jeb-kur
time	kad	kaut kad	ne-kad	jeb-kad
manner	ka	kaut ka	ne-ka	
determiner	kads, kurs	kaut kads	ne-kads	jeb-kads jeb-kurs

Cross-linguistically, interrogatives form the core of many indefinite paradigms. The Latvian 'bare' series, for example, carries the basic interrogative function, while the modified series all have other functions: the pronouns of the *kaut*-series have an existential function; the pronouns and determiners of the *ne*-series occur in the direct scope of negation; the pronouns and determiners of the *jeb*-series appear in indirect negative contexts and comparatives, and also have a free-choice interpretation.

Unlike Latvian, the various quantificational powers of Chinese *wh*-elements are not marked by distinct morphological variants.

6.4 The non-uniformity of Chinese polarity items

As the preceding chapters have shown, the various Chinese polarity items are quite distinct in both morphology and behavior. First, *renhe* differs from the *wh*-polarity items in that it can appear in the object position of a modal, which is a monotone-increasing position.

(7) Ni keyi chi pingguo → ni keyi chi shuiguo UE
   You can eat an apple. → You can eat fruit.

But even though this upward-entailing environment allows *renhe*, it cannot license *wh*-polarity items:

(8) Ni keyi zuo renhe/*shenme/*na-jian shiqing
   You can do any   what   which CL thing
   'You can do anything.'

I have suggested in previous chapters that this difference stems from the morphology of *renhe*. Recall that this pronoun contains the morpheme *ren*, meaning *wulun*. I believe it is this concessive element that allows *renhe* to be licensed in the restriction domain of *dou*, as shown below:

(9) Renhe shiqing ni dou keyi zuo
   Any thing you dou can do

'You can do anything.'
$\forall x[x\in |things| \rightarrow$ you can do x] DE

Indeed, when a similar concessive element (*wulun*) occurs with it, *shenme* can also be licensed in the object position:

(10) Ni keyi zuo wulun shenme/na-jian shiqing
You can do regardless what/which CL thing
'You can do anything.'

Taken together, these facts suggest that *ren* and *wulun*, as concessive elements, will force a universal reading on a polarity item when it occurs in the object position of a modal sentence.

6.4.1 Renhe vs. wh-*polarity items*

Then, how can we explain another frequent use of the polarity item *renhe* in Mandarin? It seems straightforward to posit that the restriction domain of conditional necessity operators is sufficient to license *renhe*. Consider the following examples, where *renhe* appears in the object and subject position, respectively:

(11) Ruguo you renhe kunnan, name women jiu xiangfangshefa zhansheng zhexie kunnan
If have *any* difficulty then we then try by hook or by crook overcome these difficulty
'If there is *any* difficulty, we will try to overcome it by hook or by crook.'

(12) Ruguo renhe kunnan cengjing dabai guo ni, ni xia-ci jiuyao gewai xiaoxin
If *any* difficulty ever beat guo you you next time then want extraordinarily be careful
'If you have been beaten by *any* difficulty, you should be extraordinarily careful of it next time.'

Sentences (11) and (12) are identical to sentences (9) and (10) except for the different polarity items they use. So, generally speaking, we can draw a natural conclusion that both *renhe* and the *wh*-indeterminate polarity items can be licensed in the antecedent clause of a bare conditional in Mandarin.

To delve deeper into a comparison of *renhe* and the *wh*-indeterminates, we need to check whether *renhe* can occur in the restriction of a *dou* sentence. Recall that this is considered a licit environment for non-interrogative *wh*-indeterminates. Here are two *dou* sentences with *renhe*:

(13) Renhe kunnan dou zudang bu zhu women yingjie xin shijie de jincheng
Any difficulty *dou* stop not stop we welcome new world de process
'*Any* difficulty cannot stop us from welcoming the new world.'

(14) renhe huanjing wenti dou shi renwei zaocheng de
any environment problem *dou* be man cause
'*Any* environmental problem is caused by human beings.'

Since we can see that the two sentences (13) and (14), which are negative and affirmative, respectively, are both grammatical, it seems clear that it is not the negative operator that licenses *renhe* as a polarity item in this context. I have argued that the real licensing condition for *renhe* is the restriction domain of the *dou* sentence itself. Consider the following sentence, which is affirmative and almost the same as the negative sentence (13):

(15) renhe kunnan dou zudang de liao zhe-ge nuoruo de nianqing-ren, ta bu-kan-yi-ji
any difficulty *dou* stop de able this weak de young man he cannot bear *any* frustration
'This weak young man can be stopped by *any* difficulty because he cannot bear *any* frustration.'

Although the negation is not the licensor in this particular situation, it still should be emphasized that, just because *dou*'s restrictor can function as a licensor for *renhe* does not mean negative sentences alone cannot license *renhe* too. In fact, the object position of a negative sentence is a very common environment for *renhe*. Consider the following sentence:

(16) wo bu chi renhe roushi
I not eat *any* meat
'I do not eat *any* kind of meat.'

Renhe in the example above is quite acceptable. On the contrary, it is not allowed in the subject position of a negative sentence. For example:

(17) *renhe roushi wo bu chi
Any meat I not eat
Intended: 'I do not eat *any* kind of meat.'

In order for *renhe* to be valid in the subject position of either a negative or affirmative sentence, it must be licensed by *dou*.

6.4.2 FCI renhe vs. NPI shenme

In addition to the object position of negative sentences and the topic position of both negative and affirmative *dou* sentences, *renhe* can also be licensed by modal verbs in Mandarin. Consider the following sentences:

(18) Women bixu zhansheng renhe kunnan
We must overcome *any* difficulty
'We must overcome *any* difficulty.'

Bixu, meaning 'must', is a human necessity operator. The example above shows that human necessity can license *renhe*. But human necessity cannot license non-interrogative *wh*-indeterminates, as shown in the following example:

(19) *Women bixu zhansheng shenme kunnan
 We must overcome what difficulty
 Intended: 'We must overcome *any* difficulty.'
(20) *Women bixu zhansheng na-ge kunnan
 We must overcome which-CL difficulty
 Intended: 'We must overcome *any* difficulty.'

Based on this evidence, we can draw a temporary conclusion: if there is no other secondary licensing condition, *renhe* can co-occur with a necessity modal in the object position, while non-interrogative *shenme* cannot. I suggest that this may be due to the different quantificational interpretation of *renhe* and *wh*-polarity items. More specifically, *renhe* is always interpreted as free choice, while *shenme* is more likely to be regarded as an existential item.

First, consider the following two sentences with *renhe*.

(21) Ni renhe shu dou keyi jie.
 You any book dou can borrow
 'You can borrow any book.'
(22) Ni keyi jie renhe shu.
 You can borrow any book
 'You can borrow any book.'

The above two sentences are semantically identical to each other; *renhe* has the same free-choice interpretation in the object position and the pre-*dou* position.

But unlike *renhe*, *shenme* in these two positions is not interchangeable.

(23) Ni shenme shu dou keyi jie.
 You what book can borrow
 'You can borrow any book.'
(24) *Ni keyi jie shenme shu.
 You can borrow what book
 Intended: 'You can borrow any book.'

I propose the following hypobook to account for this contrast: in the object position of an affirmative modal sentence, *renhe* realizes its free-choice usage, while *shenme* behaves as an NPI. But when it is fronted to a pre-*dou* position, the polarity *item* shenme becomes bound by the universal operator and so can only bear universal quantificational; thus, it can no longer function as a NPI. Thus, in affirmative modal sentences, *shenme* in object position cannot be fronted to subject position like *renhe*, because the movement invalidates its NPI interpretation.

This account seems attractive, but it may appear arbitrary in the absence of proof of *renhe*'s general preference for free-choice usage and *shenme*'s general preference for NPI usage. To seek such proof, let's examine the interaction of the two polarity items with negation. This method is used to reveal further scope differences between the two types of FCIs by Chierchia (2006). Consider a sentence like (25), for example, where negation has scope over a universal FCI. This type of sentence is typically acceptable only with the special intonation associated with the so-called 'non-rhetorical' reading (I).

(25) Wo zuotian xiawu mei kan renhe shu
 I yesterday afternoon not read any book
 I   I read some books, but I didn't read all the books. ¬∀
 II I did not read any books. ∀¬ (¬∃)

But this sentence can also express that I did not read any books (II) – that is, a non-rhetorical/NPI-like reading.

So, we can see that universal polarity items, at least in certain cases, display a scopal ambiguity vis-à-vis negation. In contrast, existential polarity items embedded under negation have only the rhetorical reading. See the following example:

(26) Wo zuotian xiawu mei kan shenme shu
 I yesterday afternoon not read what book
 I   I did not read any book ¬∃ (∀¬) NPI

This contrast shows clearly that universal FCIs and existential NPIs behave differently under negation – and this difference in behavior perfectly captures why universal *renhe* is valid when accompanied by a necessity operator, while existential *shenme* is not. This argument is based on the premise that necessity operators usually have the same quantificational power as universal operators. According to Heim (1982), the word 'must' expresses the modal relation of so-called 'human necessity'. We could recall from our earlier discussion on Heim's work which compared necessary and universal quantification. Let's simplify Kratzer's definition slightly:

(27) P is a human necessity in w with respect to R_B and $\leq o$ iff p is true in every world w' which satisfies A and B:
 A: w' R_B w
 B: for every w" R_B w: w' $\leq o$ w"

As I noted above, this definition shows that human necessity is weaker in two respects than universal quantification over the entire set of possible worlds. First, it is weaker because it ranges only over accessible worlds (that is what A says); second, it is weaker because even among the accessible worlds, it ranges only over those that are closest to the ideal (that is what B says). Thus, there exists a contrast between *renhe* and *shenme* with respect to their polarity usage when they are in the object position of sentences with *bixu*, meaning human necessity 'must'.

6.4.3 Na-*CL* vs. shenme *(bare* wh-*polarity items)*

We have seen clearly that Chinese polarity items do not behave uniformly and that there are some differences among them. For example, negation alone cannot license a non-interrogative *na*-CL construction without the help of *ye*, as mentioned before. Yet, non-interrogative *shenme phrases* can be licensed by a negative operator alone in the object position. Why should this be so?

Negative polarity items in Chinese are not homogeneous. Cheng and Giannakidou (2005, 2013) are of the opinion that Chinese FCIs should be divided into two varieties: intensional indeterminates (*na*-CL noun phrases 'which' and *renhe* noun phrases), and non-intensional ones (bare *wh*-phrases). They argue that the crucial difference between the two types of FCIs is that the former exhibit polarity behavior and are not licensed in veridical and episodic contexts, whereas the latter do not exhibit polarity behavior and are licit in episodic positive sentences. Some examples are as shown below:

(28) a *Na-ge xuesheng dou jin-lai-le
        which-CL student all enter-come-PERF
        Intended: 'Anybody/everybody came in.'
     b *Renhe ren dou jin-lai-le.
        any person all enter-come-PERF
        Intended: 'Anyone came in.'
(29) Shei dou jin-lai-le
     who all enter-come-PERF
     'Everyone came in.'

According to Cheng and Giannakidou, whether *le* is compatible with an FCI or not is a suitable indicator to show whether the FCI in question can appear in episodic positive sentences in Mandarin Chinese. Cheng and Giannakidou further argue that the contrasting distributional pattern of the two FCI varieties comes from their different behaviors in terms of intensionalization (Giannakidou, 2001; Cheng and Giannakidou, 2005, 2013). Importantly, it is the presence of a dependent world variable that renders a *wh*-phrase a polarity sensitive FCI and restricts its distribution to non-episodic contexts; on Cheng and Giannakidou's account, *na*-CL 'which' and *renhe* noun phrases contain such a variable.

Cheng and Giannakidou argue that *renhe* and *na*-CL noun phrases are of the same type in that they are both inherently intensional items. They contend that, in the case of *renhe* noun phrases, *ren* 'regardless of' provides the intensionality, while in the case of *na*-CL noun phrases, the D-linked nature of the *wh*-phrase provides the intensionality (by way of the dependent world variable). In contrast, bare *wh*-phrases such as *shenme* and *shei* are not restricted because they are not inherent intensional items. It is for this reason that Cheng and Giannakidou argue that *renhe* and *na*-CL noun phrases exhibit polarity behavior and cannot be not licensed in veridical and episodic contexts, whereas bare *wh*-phrases do not exhibit such behavior and are perfectly licit in episodic positive sentences.

However, the preceding chapters have provided significant evidence against the arguments presented by Cheng and Giannakidou. I have shown with real data and survey studies that *na*-CL polarity items *can* appear in episodic environments freely. The following episodic sentences with *na*-CLs are totally acceptable to native speakers:

(30) Na-ge xuesheng dou tongguo le kaoshi
Which-CL student *dou* pass le exam
'Every student passed the exam.'
(31) Na-ge guojia dou bu xiang zhongguo de qingkuang zheme fuza
Which-CL country *dou* not like China de situation so complicated
'The situation of China is more complicated than that of *any* other country in the world.'

In fact, the choice to draw a distinction between bare *wh*-phrases and *na*-CL noun phrases (or bare *wh*-phrases and *renhe* noun phrases) is not supported from either an empirical or theoretical perspective. If we agree with Cheng and Giannakidou that it is *ren* in *renhe* that provides intensionality, then it follows that a concessive element is the putative cause of intensionality. Yet, recall that *na*-CL noun phrases and bare *wh*-phrases are derived from *wulun ... dou ...* sentences, as I showed in the chapter on *dou*. Thus, they too have a covert or overt *wulun*, which is parallel to *ren;* if it is the *ren*-element that makes *renhe* intensional, then *na*-CL noun phrases and bare *wh*-phrases should be inherently intensional as well. Thus, the distinction between *na*-CL and *shenme* polarity items with respect to their sensitivity to intensionality seems to be exclusively theory-driven.

Still, these two *wh*-polarity items do behave differently, even if intensionality is not the culprit. What we need to do is to identify the real source of the difference between them. As we mentioned, while non-interrogative *na*-CL cannot appear in a negative sentence without an additional licensor, non-interrogative *shenme* can. For example:

(32) Ta mei kan shenme shu ?/.
He not read what book
Okay: 'What book didn't he read?'
Okay: 'He didn't read *any* book.'
(33) Ta mei kan na-ben shu?/*.
He not read which-CL book
Okay: 'Which book didn't he read?'
Not okay: Intended: 'He didn't read *any* book.'

The symbolic sequence '? /.' means the sentence it follows is grammatical when interpreted as an interrogative sentence and as a declarative one as well. The symbolic sequence '?/*.' means the sentence it follows is grammatical when interpreted as an interrogative sentence but ungrammatical when interpreted as a declarative one. The contrast shows that a *na*-CL noun phrase cannot serve as a polarity item at the sentence-final position without help from *dou*, but the bare *wh*-phrase *shenme* can.

I propose to apply the theory of (non-)D-linking to capture the distinction between *na*-CL and *shenme* in Mandarin. Cinque (1990) characterizes Pesetsky's (1987) notion of D-linking as pertaining to the relevant notion of *referentiality*, in which a phrase is D-linked if it assumes a small set of possible referents in the mind of the speaker. (Here, D denotes discourse.) According to Pesetsky, a D-linked *wh*-phrase is a *wh*-phrase whose use in a question limits the range of felicitous answers to the members of a contextually defined set; furthermore, it is reasonable to suppose that non-D-linked expressions make no such reference to contextually defined sets. However, it is not obvious that non-D-linked expressions are in any semantic or pragmatic sense 'non-referential'. Their use does not constrain the question's answer to membership in fixed sets. Thus, a *wh*-phrase such as *which man* is D-linked because it presupposes an answer from a small, pre-determined set of men, while a *wh*-element such as *who* is non-D-linked, because the answer to a question that includes interrogative *who* is not assumed to be limited to some small set of pre-determined individuals.

In Mandarin Chinese, I suggest that *na*-CL and *shenme* noun phrases are D-linked and non-D-linked, respectively, when they are used as interrogative elements; the two Chinese elements show almost no differences to their English counterparts *which* and *what* in this respect. Consider the following questions, which attempt to illustrate the (non-)D-linking properties of these two elements. In the relevant situation, two friends are talking about recent best-sellers in the classroom. One says to the other:

(34) zuijin shenme shu zui liuxing?
 recent what book most popular
 'What book is most popular recently?'
(35) zuijin na-ben shu zui liuxing?
 recent which-CL book most popular
 'Which book is most popular recently?'

If the speaker uses '*shenme shu*', he indicates no expectation as to the identity of the recent best-seller. If, on the other hand, the speaker uses '*na-ben shu*', he is assuming that the best-seller in question belongs to some con0textually defined set salient in his interlocutor's awareness (for example, a shelf of twelve books the two friends are looking at in the classroom). Therefore, in the second case, the noun phrase expected as an answer to the question should select an unidentified member of that set.

Given this contrast, it is not surprising that *na*-CL and bare *shenme* are D-linked and non-D-linked, respectively, when they appear in their interrogative uses. What I want to emphasize here is that their *polarity* use inherits some properties of their interrogative use – including the property of being D-linked and non-D-linked, respectively.

Specifically, I propose that *na-ge ren*, when used as a polarity item (in parallel with *which man*), presupposes an existential given set of human beings. Conversely, *shenme ren*, when used as a polarity item (in parallel with *what man*), does not presuppose an existential given set of human beings. Consider the following conversation: in this scenario, two editors are talking about some news concerning recent best-sellers in the market. One says to the other:

(36) xianzai shichang hen huo, shenme shu dou mai de hen hao.
Now market very hot what book *dou* sell de very good
'The market environment is good nowadays; all books sell well.'
(37) Xianzai shichang hen huo, na-ben shu dou mai de hen hao.
Now market very hot which-CL book *dou* sell de very good
'The market environment is good nowadays; all books sell well.'

If the speaker uses '*shenme shu*', he indicates no expectation as to the identity of the books which sell well these days. If, on the other hand, the speaker uses '*na-ben shu*', he is assuming that the best-sellers in question belong to some contextually defined set salient in his interlocutor's awareness. Therefore, in the second case, the noun phrase uttered by the speaker and heard by the hearer refers to an identified set of books which is familiar (or just known by) the two editors.

However, the distinction between *na*-CL noun phrases and *shenme* noun phrases with respect to their D-linking or non-D-linking property is not sufficient to account for their different behavior as polarity items in sentence-final position in a straightforward way. To account for this behavior, we need the help of a supplementary theory of information structure.

According to Krifka (2006), the sentence-final position prefers to accommodate new information, while the sentence-initial position prefers to accommodate given information. Consider the following examples, drawn from Krifka (2006):

(38) a   Bill showed the boy a girl.
     b   * Bill showed a boy the girl.
     c   Bill showed the girl to a boy.

The definite article is commonly said to differ from the indefinite article in that, when the former heads a noun phrase, the resulting interpretation is a *given* denotation, whereas when the latter heads a noun phrase, the resulting interpretation is a relatively *new* denotation. When the two kinds of noun phrases are combined in a ditransitive construction like the one in (12), the indefinite noun phrase prefers to follow, not to precede, the definite one. Likewise, in Mandarin, *na*-CL polarity items that presuppose an existential given set of individuals prefer the sentence-initial position, whereas interrogative *na*-CL constructions that bring in new information prefer the sentence-final position. However, as a non-D-linked phrase, a *shenme* noun phrase has no such preference.

Given the distinction between *na*-CL and *shenme* polarity items with respect to their D-linking or non-D-linking properties, we may predict that if we provide some information about the antecedent of a polarity item, *na*-CL can be licensed in a near-sentence-final position. This kind of information is not necessarily provided by the occurrence of an overt antecedent set, such as the one illustrated in (39).

(39) Nimen ziji zuozhu, wo bu neng daiti na-ge ren zuo jueding
You-selves decide I *ye* not can replace which-CL de decision
'You take the responsibility for your own decisions. I cannot make the decision for any one of you.'

Na-ge ren in the sentence above expresses a free choice among human beings. But it still imposes a limit that the hearer must observe when interpreting the polarity item; that is, the choice must be made among the set of individuals denoted by *nimen* 'you'. Since the first clause sets up this context cue for the second clause, *na*-ge ren in such a situation can be situated near the sentence-final position. The same point can be illustrated by a scenario that provides an overall background for the denotation of a *na*-CL noun phrase, like the situation in (40).

(40) Zhongguo xianzai qingkuang hen fuza, meiti hennan shuo qingchu na-jian shiqing de zhenxiang
China now situation very complicated media hard tell clear which-CL thing de truth
'The situation of China nowadays is complicated. It's hard for the media to tell the truth of anything in this country.'

6.5 The contribution of *ye*

So far in this chapter, I have accounted for the difference between *na*-CL and *shenme* noun phrases and used the distinction between them to account for the puzzle of why *na*-CL noun phrases cannot be licensed in sentence-final position in a negative declarative sentence by applying an analysis based on information theory. Specifically, when investigating the use of *na*-CL and *shenme* noun phrases in 'a negative declarative sentence', I was looking exclusively at sentences without *dou*. The reason for this is that I consider *dou* to function as the licensor for Mandarin polarity items whenever it appears, even if there is also a negative operator in the same clause – because, as we have seen in the previous discussion, I contend that the real factor affecting the appearance of non-interrogative *na*-CL noun phrases in *dou* sentences is the downward-entailing property of *dou*'s restrictor, not the negation itself.

Negation, however, *can* license *na*-CL noun phrases as polarity items in the absence of *dou*. Consider the following example:

(41) Na-bu dianying ye buneng/meiyou chaoyue luanshi jiaren zai wo xinmu zhong de diwei
Which-CL movie *ye* cannot not exceed gone with the wind at my mind de status
'There is no movie that can exceed *Gone with the Wind* in my mind.'

Dou is replaced by *ye* in this sentence.

A new question naturally arises from this discussion. That is, if *na*-CL polarity items are already licensed by negation and the sentence-initial position give preference to *na*-CL noun phrases as the sentential topic (where *topic* is defined as a position for given information, met in this case by the D-linked status of a *na*-CL *wh*-phrase), why can these two conditions together not make a non-interrogative *na*-CL noun phrase appear licit? For illustration of the ungrammaticality of this situation, see the following example. This sentence is unacceptable if *ye* is omitted:

(42) Zheci chehuo zhong na-wei chengke *(ye) mei neng cunhuo xialai
 This time traffic accident inside which-CL passenger *(*ye*) not can survive down
 'No passenger survived in this traffic accident.'

In the situation illustrated in (42), negation takes responsibility for licensing *na-wei chengke* as a polarity item. However, it appears that *ye* has its own contribution to offer in this case. As we have seen in the preceding discussion, the reason why the downward-entailing environment can license polarity items is that polarity items in such contexts can give birth to stronger statements. This is where *ye* comes in. With the help of the particle *ye*, the domain-widening function of *na-wei chengke* in the negation context serves to strengthen the statement overall, which satisfies the licensing requirement of the polarity item according to the downward-entailing approach (Kadmon and Landman, 1993, and others). Thus, it may express, for example, that all passengers died *including even* the ones who sat beside the window and were most likely to escape from the traffic accident.

Ye, in this strengthening function, is much the same as the English particle *even*, which is regarded as carrying part of the lexical meaning of polarity items by a lot of researchers (Lee and Horn, 1994; Krifka, 1995; Lahiri, 1998). According to these scholars, a phrase with *even* picks out the least likely individual from a given set of alternatives. Likelihood here is understood as a possibility scale in the sense of Horn (1972, 1989). When combined with ONE in a positive sentence, the low likelihood property of *even* will yield oddity, if not total ungrammaticality. With negation, on the other hand, *even* plus a polarity item will be acceptable, since the negative context will satisfy the low likelihood property of *even*.

I propose that the focus-sensitive operator of negative polarity *na*-CL is syntactically realized by *ye* in Mandarin; in other languages, similar operators are often realized morphologically, as in Hindi (Lahiri, 1998), or covertly, as in English (Krifka, 1995).

It should be further noted that *na*-CL in such cases is not allowed in the post-*ye* position. It can only occur in the pre-*ye* position, even if there is some contextual information available about the antecedent of the *na*-CL noun phrase.

(43) Na-ge ren de jueding wo ye bu neng yingxiang
 Which-CL man de decision I *ye* not can affect
 'I cannot affect anyone's decision.'

(44) Nimen zhexie haizi, *wo ye bu neng yingxiang na-ge ren de jueding
You these children I *ye* not can affect which-CL man de decision
Intended: 'I cannot affect anyone's decision for you children.'

This does not mean, however, that *na*-CL noun phrases are absolutely excluded from the post-*ye* position. In fact, they *can* appear after *ye* – provided they are not licensed by *ye*. In the following case, non-interrogative *na-ge ren* is licensed by negation, assisted by contextual information provided by the first clause. The appearance of *ye*, in this case, has nothing to do with non-interrogative *na-ge ren*, but serves as a focus-sensitive operator which influences the adjacent focus element *wo* 'I'.

(45) Nimen zhexie haizi, wo ye bu neng yingxiang na-ge ren de jueding
You these children I *ye* not can affect which-CL man de decision
'Even I (as your mother) cannot affect someone's decision for you kids.'

The contrast between (44) and (45) not only suggests that non-interrogative *na*-CL noun phrases cannot be licensed in a post-*ye* position, but also shows the different quantificational powers of non-interrogative *na*-CL noun phrases when they are licensed by different operators. Comparing the intended meaning of (44) and the actual meaning of (45), we can see that *na*-CL noun phrases show universal quantification when licensed by a pre-*ye* position, on the one hand, and show existential quantification when licensed by a negative operator, on the other hand. They thus function as free-choice items and negative polarity items in those two kinds of contexts, respectively. We can use the 'absolutely' diagnostic to support this argument. Recall that *almost* – along with such similar adverbs as *nearly* and *absolutely* – can modify universal operators, but not existential or other non-universal operators. The counterparts of *almost* in Mandarin are *chabuduo* and *jihu*. As expected, *chabuduo* and *jihu* can co-occur with a free-choice *na*-CL noun phrase, but not with negative polarity *na*-CL noun phrase. Consider the examples in (39) and (45), where *na-ge ren* serves as a free-choice item in the former sentence but a negative polarity item in the latter one. *Jihu* can only appear licit in the former sentence, as the following two examples illustrate.

(46) Nimen ziji zuozhu, wo jihu bu neng daiti na-ge ren zuo jueding
You-selves decide I almost *ye* not can replace which-CL de decision
'You take the responsibility for your own decisions. I almost cannot make the decision for any one of you.'
(47) *Nimen zhexie haizi, wo ye jihu bu neng yingxiang na-ge ren de jueding
You these children I *ye* almost not can affect which-CL man de decision
Intended: 'Even I (as your mother) almost cannot affect someone's decision for you children.'

Ye is associated with *na-ge ren* 'which man' in sentence (39) and with *wo* 'I' in sentence (45). If we understand *ye* to function like a concentrator which serves to centralize the hearer's attention on some issue in focus, it must emphasize *na-ge ren* and *wo*, respectively, in the two sentences. It emphasizes the element in focus by making the focus introduce alternatives. So, for example, in sentence (39), *ye* causes *wo* to introduce alternatives; it has nothing to do with the domain widening of *na-ge ren* 'which-man' among the children, but instead emphasizes that the speaker herself is the least likely person to be unable to affect the decisions of her children. But for sentence (45), *ye* is focus-sensitive to *na-ge ren*, so it makes *na-ge ren* introducing alternatives. The emphasizing function of *ye*, in this case, serves to widen the domain of *na-ge ren* so that it embraces even the marginal members of *ren* 'men'.

It should be emphasized once again that *ye* and negation cannot license non-interrogative *na*-CL noun phrases by themselves. A pre-*ye* position in a negative sentence, however, is an acceptable environment for non-interrogative *na*-CL noun phrases. Although negation is a typical downward-entailing context, it cannot license *na*-CL noun phrases without the help of *ye*. If *ye* does not appear, there needs to be previous contextual information establishing the *na*-CL polarity item in a negative sentence; this is the case where the D-linked property of the *na*-CL noun phrase and information structure comes into play.

Although the various quantificational powers of Chinese *wh*-elements are not marked by distinct morphological variants, they do behave differently. This chapter focuses on the distinction between *renhe* and wh-polarity items, arguing that the contrast between these two types of elements shows clearly that universal free-choice items and existential negative polarity items behave differently under negation – and this difference in behavior perfectly captures why universal *renhe* is valid when accompanied by a necessity operator, while existential *shenme* is not (since human necessity is weaker than universal quantification over the entire set of possible worlds). This chapter also applies the theory of (non-)D-linking to capture the distinction between *na*-CL and *shenme* in Mandarin when these two elements are used as polarity items.

7 Conclusions

Studies of polarity items have traditionally fallen into two major theoretical camps: the downward entailment approach, and the non-veridicality approach. In line with the second approach, previous studies on Chinese polarity items have treated non-veridicality as the licensor of polarity items, as elaborated in Lin (1998)'s *non-entailment-of-existence condition*, Li (1992)'s *non-positively-fixed truth condition* and the reformulation of the above-mentioned two conditions in Cheng and Giannakidou (2005, 2013). Departing from this previous body of research on Chinese polarity items, the current study employs Ladusaw (1979)'s downward entailment hypothesis, rather than the non-veridicality hypothesis, as its analytical foundation. Based on a close and systematic examination of Chinese polarity items, I have drawn together several pieces of evidence to argue that non-veridicality is neither a necessary nor sufficient condition for licensing polarity items and thus offers inferior explanatory power in comparison to the downward entailment hypothesis.

An important issue addressed in this book is the status of the element *dou* that often co-occurs with Chinese polarity items. The explanation for why some Chinese polarity items must be licensed by the element *dou* has yet to receive sufficient attention in the literature, and thus warrants further study. While it is clear that the pre-*dou* position is a very common environment for Chinese polarity items, it is less clear why this position is a licit environment for polarity items: these *dou* sentences are not always non-veridical, and most of them, to our knowledge, are obviously affirmative utterances with the typical episodic marker *le*.

Following previous research by Pan (2006), the present book argues that the element *dou* carries a universal operator function, which can introduce a tripartite structure carrying two unequal arguments – the restriction domain and the nuclear scope, respectively, each of which is filled by different components of the *dou* sentence. Building on this tripartite structure analysis, I claim that the crucial licensing condition for Chinese polarity items in *dou* sentences is the downward-entailing property of *dou*'s restriction domain. Not only does this analysis provide strong support for the downward-entailing approach to polarity items generally, but it also allows us to account for the co-occurrence of *dou* and polarity items in Mandarin under the frame of the downward entailment approach.

Conclusions   115

Having already been refuted by Horn (2000), the non-veridicality approach to polarity items is further challenged by the Mandarin Chinese data provided in this study. Due to its explanatory inadequacy, I discard the non-veridicality approach and rely instead on the traditional downward entailment approach. I consistently adopt this approach in accounting for Chinese polarity phenomena in this book; I argue for a uniform treatment of all Chinese polarity phenomena, according to which polarity items must be licensed in a downward-entailing environment.

A crucial requirement of this analysis is that we specify the level on which monotonicity is checked. I argue that downward entailment is not checked on the surface level or any other linguistic level, but at Logical Form, where domain widening applies. Sometimes, the particular context of domain widening happens to also be downward entailing on the surface level; sometimes, it does not. Fortunately, the tripartite structure allows us to focus only on the fundamental properties that the linguistic structures have in common, rather than the linguistic structures themselves. Thus, specifying the level at which downward entailment should be assessed helps solve the problem presented by sentences for which the monotonicity of the restriction domain of the tripartite structure is not identical to the monotonicity of the surface position in which the polarity item appears.

Relegating the satisfaction of downward entailment to the level of Logical Form also helps solve a problem with regard to sentences like the following: *Only John ate any vegetable for breakfast*. Sentences like this are okay, grammatically speaking; however, they pose a problem for the downward entailment approach because the object position does not appear to be a downward-entailing context (since it does not allow inference from the general interpretation to the specific interpretation). Von Fintel (1999) proposes a solution to this problem: he suggests that, when we assess entailment, we must automatically include the presuppositions of the conclusion in the entailment's premise. As soon as the presupposition of the sentence *Only John ate any vegetable for breakfast* is included in the assessment of the entailment, the inference proceeds smoothly.

However, I show that the tripartite structure analysis employed in this study offers a simpler, better solution to this problem. If we formalize this sentence in question as a tripartite structure, $\forall x[x$ ate vegetable for breakfast $\to x = $ John], we can see that the position licensing *any* occupies the downward-entailment restriction domain of a universal operator. Once again, an apparent problem for the downward entailment approach can be straightforwardly accounted for within the downward entailment framework by appealing to tripartite structures. Simpler and neater than von Fintel's approach, this tripartite structure analysis is also more attractive in cases where von Fintel's argument fails, since not every sentence holds an appropriate presupposition. Finally, there is another pleasant by-product of this tripartite structure analysis: the coercive co-occurrence of the classifiers *dianr* and *ge* with *shenme* in some episodic sentences has long been noticed by scholars, but no convincing account for this phenomenon has been provided based on the non-veridicality account of polarity items. The tripartite structure solution proposed in the current study offers a satisfactory explanation for this phenomenon, and provides another piece of evidence for the downward entailment approach.

Three kinds of polarity items in Mandarin Chinese – *shenme, na*-CL and *renhe* – are taken into consideration in this study. These three kinds of polarity items behave rather differently from one another with respect to their polarity sensitivity. Based on the discrepancies in their distribution, I argue that the three kinds of polarity items can be divided into two groups – those with a concessive element *ren*, and those without such an element. The former group has *renhe* as its only member, while the latter group comprises *shenme* and *na*-CL. The division I propose is different from the one previously proposed by Cheng and Giannakidou, who assess the non-interrogative *na*-CL and *renhe* as one group and *shenme* as the other. I show that the classification I propose fits the linguistic facts much better and provides another piece of evidence against the analysis of Cheng and Giannakidou.

Finally, an important generalization can be drawn about the different patterns of behavior between these two groups of polarity items: all the environments that license non-interrogative *shenme* and *na*-CL constructions also license *renhe* as a polarity item, but not vice versa. I argue that this behavioral asymmetry reflects the fact that, in contrast with the *wh*-polarity items *shenme* and *na*-CL, the distribution of *renhe* is much wider – it can be licensed by human necessity and possibility, in addition to conditional necessity. I present a thorough comparison among these three kinds of polarity items in Mandarin Chinese, identifying a further difference between *renhe* and the *wh*-polarity items, which I argue arises due to a morphological difference between them: specifically, I propose that *renhe*, as a universal quantifier, is used in free-choice indefinite contexts, whereas *shenme*, as an existential quantifier, is used primarily in negative polarity contexts. Finally, I argue that the difference between *na*-CL and *shenme* is caused by the fact that the former is a D-linking element, while the latter is not.

References

Beaver, D., and Clark, B. (2003). Always and only: Why not all focus-sensitive operators are alike. *Natural Language Semantics*, *11*(4), pp. 323–362.
Beaver, D., and Clark, B. (2008). *Sense and Sensitivity: How Focus Determines Meaning*. London: Wiley-Blackwell.
Carlson, G. N. (1980). Polarity any is existential. *Linguistic Inquiry*, *11*(4), pp. 799–804.
Carlson, G. N. (1981). Distribution of free choice any. *Proceedings of the Chicago Linguistic Society*, *17*, pp. 8–23.
Cheng, L.-S. (1991). On the typology of wh-questions. PhD. Massachusetts Institute of Technology.
Cheng, L.-S. (2009). On every type of quantificational expression in Chinese. *Quantification, Definiteness, and Nominalisation*, pp. 53–75.
Cheng, L.-S., and Giannakidou, A. (2005). The non-uniformity of wh-indeterminates with free choice in Chinese. In Tsoulas, G. and K.-H. Gil (eds), *The Nature of Quantification and Crosslinguistic Variation*, pp. 123–154. Oxford: Oxford University Press.
Cheng, L.-S., and Giannakidou, A. (2013). The non-uniformity of wh-indeterminates with free choice in Chinese. *Strategies of Quantification*, pp. 123–151.
Cheng, L.-S., and Huang, C. T. J. (1996). Two types of donkey sentences. *Natural Language Semantics*, *4*(2), pp. 121–163.
Chierchia, G. (2004). Scalar implicatures, polarity phenomena, and the syntax/pragmatics interface. In A. Belletti (ed.), *The Cartography of Syntactic Structures*. Vol. 3: *Structures and Beyond*. Oxford: Oxford University Press.
Chierchia, G. (2006). Broaden your views: Implicatures of domain widening and the 'logicality' of language. *Linguistic Inquiry*, *37*(4), pp. 535–590.
Chierchia, G. (2013). *Logic in Grammar: Polarity, Free Choice, and Intervention*. Oxford: Oxford University Press.
Cinque, G. (1990). *Types of A'-Dependencies*. Cambridge, MA: MIT Press.
Dayal, V. (1998). Any as inherently modal. *Linguistics and Philosophy*, *21*(5), pp. 433–476.
Diesing, M. (1992). Bare plural subjects and the derivation of logical representations. *Linguistic Inquiry*, *23*(3), pp. 353–380.
Ding, S.-S. et al. (1961). *Xiandai Hanyu Yufa Jianghua*. Beijing: The Commercial Press.
Dowty, D. (1994). The role of negative polarity and concord marking in natural language reasoning. *Proceedings of Semantics and Linguistic Theory*, *4*, pp. 114–144.
Eisner, J. (1994). '$\forall$'-less in wonderland? Revisiting any. ESCOL 11, Proceedings of the Eleventh Eastern States Conference on Linguistics, DMLL, Department of Modern Languages and Linguistics, Cornell University, pp. 92–103.

References

Fauconnier, G. (1975). Polarity and the scale principle. *Chicago Linguistic Society*, *11*, pp. 188–199.

Fauconnier, G. (1979). Implication reversal in a natural language. In F. Guenthner and S. Schmidt (eds.), *Formal Semantics and Pragmatics for Natural Languages*, pp. 289–301. Dordrecht: Reidel.

Fauconnier, G. (1980). Pragmatic entailment and questions. In J. R. Searle, F. Kiefer, and M. Bierwisch (eds.), *Speech Act Theory and Pragmatics*, pp. 57–69. Dordrecht: Reidel.

Feng, Y.-L. (2014). A semantic study of distributive effects in Mandarin in Chinese. PhD. City University of Hong Kong.

Gajewski, J. R. (2010). Superlatives, npis and most. *Journal of Semantics*, *27*(1), pp. 125–137.

Giannakidou, A. (1994). The semantic licensing of NPIs and the Modern Greek subjunctive. In *Language and Cognition 4, Yearbook of the Research Group for Theoretical and Experimental Linguistics*, pp. 55–68. Groningen, Netherlands: University of Groningen.

Giannakidou, A. (1997). The landscape of polarity items. PhD. University of Groningen.

Giannakidou, A. (1998). *Polarity Sensitivity as (Non)veridical Dependency*. Amsterdam: John Benjamins.

Giannakidou, A. (1999). Affective dependencies. *Linguistics and Philosophy*, *22*(4), pp. 367–421.

Giannakidou, A. (2001). The meaning of free choice. *Linguistics and Philosophy*, *24*(6), pp. 659–735.

Giannakidou, A. (2006). Only, emotive factive verbs, and the dual nature of polarity dependency. *Language*, *82*(3), pp. 575–603.

Giannakidou, A. (2008). Negative and positive polarity items: Variation, licensing, and compositionality. In C. Maienborn, H. von Klaus, and P. Portner (eds.), *Semantics: An International Handbook of Natural Language Meaning*. Berlin: Mouton de Gruyter.

Giannakidou, A., and Cheng, L.-S. (2006). (In)definiteness, polarity, and the role of wh-morphology in free choice. *Journal of Semantics*, *23*(2), pp. 135–183.

Guo, J., and Lee, P.-L. (2016). A semantic account of *zong* and *zongshi* in mandarin Chinese. *IACL*, *24*.

Hackl, M. (2009). On the grammar and processing of proportional quantifiers: Most versus more than half. *Natural Language Semantics*, *17*(1), pp. 63–98.

Hajičová, E., Partee, B. H., and Sgall, P. (1998). *Topic-Focus Articulation, Tripartite Structures, and Semantic Content*. Netherlands: Springer.

Hamblin, C. L. (1973). Questions in montague English. *Montague Grammar*, *10*(1), pp. 41–53.

Han, C. H., and Laura, S. (1996). Syntactic and semantic conditions on NPI licensing in questions. Proceedings of the Fifteenth Qest Coast Conference on Formal Linguistics. Standford, Palo Alto.

Haspelmath, B. M. (1997). *Indefinite pronouns*. Oxford: Oxford University Press.

Heim, I. (1982). The semantics of definite and indefinite noun phrases. PhD. University of Massachusetts, Amherst.

Heim, I. (1984). A note on negative polarity and downward entailingness. *Proceedings of NELS*, *14*, pp. 98–107.

Hoeksema, J. (2000). Negative polarity items: Triggering, scope, and c-command. *Negation and Polarity: Syntactic and Semantic Perspectives*, pp. 115–146.

Horn, L. R. (1972). On the semantic properties of logical operators in English. PhD. University of California, Los Angeles.

Horn, L. R. (1989). *A Natural History of Negation*. Chicago: Chicago University Press.

References

Horn, L. R. (1996). Exclusive company: Only and the dynamics of vertical inference. *Journal of Semantics*, 13, pp. 1–40.

Horn, L. R. (1997). All John's children are as bald as the King of France: Existential import and the geometry of opposition. *Chicago Linguistics Society*, 33, pp. 155–179.

Horn, L. R. (1999). Any and (-)ever: Free choice and free relatives. Paper presented at Israel Association for Theoretical Linguistics (IATL) 15, Haifa.

Horn, L. R. (2000). Pick a theory: Not just any theory: Indiscriminatives and the free-choice indefinite. In L. Horn and Y. Kato (eds.), *Negation and Polarity: Syntactic and Semantic Perspectives*, pp. 147–192. Oxford: Oxford University Press.

Huang, J. -T. (1982). Logical relations in Chinese and the theory of grammar. PhD. MIT.

Israel, M. (1996). Polarity sensitivity as lexical semantics. *Linguistics and Philosophy*, 19(6), pp. 619–666.

Israel, M. (2004). The pragmatics of polarity. In L. Horn and G. Ward (eds.), *The Handbook of Pragmatics*, pp. 701–723. Oxford: Blackwell.

Jiang, Y. (1998). The pragmatical inference and the syntax and semantics to *dou*. *Xiandai Waiyu*, 1, pp. 12–24.

Jiang, Y. (2015). Dou yunzhun renxuanci de liju. *Daidai xiucixue*, 5, pp. 11–34.

Kadmon, N., and Landman, F. (1993). Any. *Linguistics and Philosophy*, 16, pp. 353–422.

Kas, M. (1993). Essays on Boolean functions and negative polarity. *Groningen Dissertations in Linguistics* 11, Groningen.

Kato, Y. (2000). Interpretive asymmetries in negation. In L. Horn and Y. Kato (eds.), *Negation and Polarity: Syntactic and Semantic Perspectives*, pp. 62–87. Oxford: Oxford University Press.

Klima, E. (1964). *Negation in English: In the Structure of Language*. Englewood Cliffs: Prentice-Hall.

Kratzer, A. (2005). Indefinites and the operators they depend on: From Japanese to salish1. Reference and Quantification: The Partee Effect. CSLI Publications, Stanford.

Kratzer, A., and Shimoyama, J. (2002). Indeterminate Pronouns: The View from Japanese. Tokyo Conference on Psycholinguist ICS.

Krifka, M. (1995). The semantics and pragmatics of polarity. *Linguistic Analysis*, 15, pp. 209–257.

Krifka, M. (2006). The notions of information structure. *Interdisciplinary Studies on Information Structure*, 6. 10.1556/ALing.55.2008.3-4.2.

Kroch, A. (1972). The semantics of scope in English. PhD. MIT.

Kuo, C.-M. (2003). The fine structure of negative polarity items in Chinese. PhD. University of Southern California.

Kuroda, S.-Y. (1965). Generative grammatical studies in the Japanese language. PhD. MIT.

Ladusaw, W. A. (1979). Polarity sensitivity as inherent scope relations. PhD. University of Texas, Austin.

Ladusaw, W. A. (1996). Negation and polarity items. In L. Shalom (ed.), *The Handbook of Contemporary Semantic Theory*, pp. 321–341. Oxford: Blackwell Publishing Ltd.

Lahiri, U. (1998). Focus and negative polarity in Hindi. *Natural Language Semantics*, 6, pp. 57–125.

Laka, I. (1990). Negation in syntax: On the nature of functional categories and projections. PhD. MIT, Cambridge, MA.

Lee, C. (1996). Negative polarity items in English and Korean. *Language Sciences*, 18(1–2), pp. 505–523.

Lee, Y.-S., and Horn, L. R. (1994). Any as an indefinite plus even. Unpublished MS. Yale University, New Haven, CT.

LeGrand, J. E. (1975). Or and any: The semantics and syntax of two logical operators. PhD. University of Chicago, Chicago.
Li, Y. H. A. (1992). Indefinite wh, in mandarin chinese. *Journal of East Asian Linguistics*, *1*(2), pp. 125–155.
Liao, H.-C. (2011). Alternatives and exhaustification: Non-interrogative uses of Chinese wh-words. PhD. Harvard University, Cambridge, MA.
Lin, J.-W. (1996). Polarity licensing and wh-phrase quantification in Chinese. PhD. University of Massachusetts Amherst.
Lin, J.-W. (1998). On existential polarity wh-phrases in Chinese. *Journal of East Asian Linguistics*, *7*(3), pp. 219–255.
Linebarger, M. C. (1980). The grammar of negative polarity. PhD. MIT., Cambridge, MA.
Linebarger, M. C. (1981). Polarity any as an existential quantifier. *Proceedings of the Chicago Linguistics Society*, *16*, pp. 211–219.
Linebarger, M. C. (1987). Negative polarity and grammatical representation. *Linguistics and Philosophy*, *10*(3), pp. 325–387.
Lü, S.-X. (1980). *Jindai Hanyu Zhidaici*. Beijing: The Commercial Press.
Montague, R. (1969). On the nature of certain philosophical entities. *The Monist*, *53*(2), pp. 159–194.
Nishigauchi, T. (1986). *Quantification in Syntax*. PhD. University of Massachusetts, Amherst.
Nishigauchi, T. (1990). *Quantification in the Theory of Grammar*. Dordrecht: Kluwer Academic.
Pan, H.-H. (2006). *Focus, Tripartite and the Interpretation of Dou*. Yufa Yanjiu yu Tansuo 13. Beijing: The Commercial Press.
Partee, B. H. (1987). Noun Phrase interpretation and type-shifting principles. In J. A. G. Groenendijk, D. D. Jongh, and M. B. J. Stokhof (eds.), *Studies in Discourse, Representation Theory and the Theory of Generalized Quantifiers*, pp. 115–143. Dordrecht: Foris.
Partee, B. H. (1995). Quantificational structures and compositionality. In E. Bach, E. Jelinek, A. Kratzer, and B. H. Partee (eds.). *Quantification in Natural Language*. Vol. II, pp. 541–601. Dordrecht: Kluwer.
Pesetsky, D. (1987). Wh-in-situ: Movement and unselective binding. In Reuland, E., A. G. B. ter Meulen (eds.), *The Representation of in Definiteness*. Cambridge, MA: MIT Press.
Progovac, L. (1993). Negative polarity: Entailment and binding. *Linguistics and Philosophy*, *16*(2), pp. 149–180.
Progovac, L. (1994). *Positive and Negative Polarity: A Binding Approach*. Cambridge: Cambridge University Press.
Reichenbach, H. (1947). Elements of symbolic logic. *Journal of Symbolic Logic*, *31*(4), pp. 201–212.
Rooth, M. (1985). Association with focus. PhD. University of Massachusetts, Amherst.
Rullmann, H. (1996). Two types of negative polarity items. In K. Kusumoto et al. (eds.), *Proceedings of NELS 26*, pp. 335–350. Amherst, MA: GLSA.
Schwarzschild, R. (1996). *Pluralities*. Dordrecht: Kluwer Academic.
Shao, J. M. (1996). *Xiandai Hanyu Yiwenju Yanjiu*. Shanghai: East China Normal University Press.
Stalnaker, R. (1978). Assertion. In *Syntax and Semantics 9: Pragmatics*, pp. 315–332. New York: Academic Press.
Szabolcsi, A., Bott, L., and Mcelree, B. (2008). The effect of negative polarity items on inference verification. *Journal of Semantics*, *25*(4), pp. 411–450.
von Fintel, K. (1999). NPI-licensing, Strawson-entailment, and context-dependency. *Journal of Semantics*, *8*(2), pp. 97–148.

Wouden, T. V. D. (1997). Negative contexts: Collocation, polarity and multiple negation. *Language*, *75*(3), p. 589.

Wu, Y.-Q. (2000). Danweici shi Jiduan WH+Cixiang de Yunzhun. *XiandaiWaiyu*, *4*, pp. 383–393.

Xiang, M. (2008). Plurality, maximality and scalar inferences: A case study of mandarin dou. *Journal of East Asian Linguistics*, *17*(3), pp. 227–245.

Xiang, Y.-M. (2016). Questions with non-exhaustive answers. PhD. Harvard University, Cambridge, MA.

Yu, X.-L. (1965). Yiwen Daici de Renzhi Yongfa. *Zhongguo Yuwen*, *1*, pp. 30–36.

Yuan, Y.-L. (2007). Lun dou de yinxing fouding he jixiang Yunzhun Gongneng. *Zhongguo Yuwen*, *4*, pp. 306–320.

Zwarts, F. (1993). Three types of polarity, Ms. Also appeared as Zwarts (1998). In F. Hamn and E. Hinrichs (eds.), *Plural Quantification*. Dordrecht: Kluwer.

Zwarts, F. (1995). Nonveridical contexts. *Linguistic Analysis*, *25*(3), pp. 286–312.

Index

alternative 7, 8, 9, 13, 19, 36, 40, 43, 48, 49, 50, 54, 64, 66, 68, 73, 74, 79, 83, 88, 99, 100, 111, 113
any 1–2, 4–10, 12, 13, 15, 16, 21–26, 47, 51, 52, 67, 68, 75, 77, 100, 115

Chierchia, G. 7, 8, 11, 13, 105
conditional 10, 13, 15, 21, 33, 46, 62, 63, 71, 79–81, 87–97, 102, 116

domain widening 1, 5–8, 36, 83, 111, 113, 115
downward-entailing 3–5, 9, 16, 19, 20, 23–25, 30, 34–36, 54, 56, 58, 67, 68, 70, 72, 73–75, 77–79, 82, 83, 93, 97, 110–115

entailment 1, 3, 4, 10, 11, 15, 19, 27, 33, 36, 56, 58, 67, 68, 70–72, 75–77, 79, 81, 83, 91, 94, 95, 114–116
ever 5, 12, 13, 23, 57, 68, 70, 72, 80
every 4, 22, 59, 68
existential 8–10, 14, 15, 17–21, 23, 32, 39, 67, 73, 98, 99, 101, 104, 105, 109, 112, 113, 116

focus 7–9, 13, 36, 38, 40, 43, 48–50, 52, 53–57, 65–66, 72–73, 74, 77, 83, 99, 100, 111–112, 113
free choice 5, 7–10, 13–16, 21, 27–29, 46, 47, 56, 58, 62, 67, 98, 100, 101, 104, 110, 112, 113, 116

generic 7, 10, 13, 15, 21, 30, 32–34, 98
Giannakidou, A. 2–4, 10–12, 22, 24, 25, 27–30, 33, 36–39, 42, 57, 67, 94, 106, 107, 114, 116

Heim, I. 3, 17, 61, 64, 85–90, 92, 95, 99, 105, 116
Horn, L. 1, 8, 9, 11, 14, 15, 21, 36, 51, 52, 55, 67, 74, 83, 100, 111, 115

Krifka, M. 7, 8, 11, 12, 24, 83, 100, 109, 111

Ladusaw, W. 1–5, 11, 14, 15, 68, 69, 114
Lahiri, U. 1, 3, 7–9, 11, 83, 100, 111
licensing condition 16, 25, 26, 31, 33, 36, 37, 58, 67, 84, 89, 91, 93, 96, 97, 103, 104, 114

modal 13–16, 19, 21, 22, 29, 31, 32, 35, 37, 64, 65, 79, 85–97, 101–105

necessity 26, 67, 79, 80, 84, 97, 102, 104, 105, 113, 116
negative polarity 1, 5, 7–10, 13–17, 20–24, 38, 52, 56, 58, 67, 70, 83, 84, 98, 100, 106, 111, 112, 113

quantification 15, 34, 42, 43–45, 49, 50, 56, 64, 80, 84–89, 94, 95, 98, 99, 105, 112, 113
quantifier 7, 14, 15, 17, 22, 23, 35, 37, 39, 43, 59, 60, 79, 87, 97, 116

scalar 8, 14, 15, 24, 37, 50–53, 100
set 4, 6, 8, 9, 11, 13, 15, 27, 29, 33, 38, 46, 48–50, 54, 55, 60, 61, 63, 64, 66–69, 71, 74, 75, 82, 83, 85, 86, 94, 95, 99, 100, 105, 108, 109–111, 113
strength 19, 88

tripartite structure 4, 57–59, 61, 63, 64–67, 71, 73–75, 77–81, 83–85, 94, 97, 114–115

universal 1, 7, 13–17, 21–23, 25, 26, 32–35, 37–40, 42–46, 49, 52, 53, 55, 56, 60, 65, 66, 70, 71, 73, 74, 77–80, 87–89, 92–99, 102, 104, 105, 112–116
upward-entailing 3, 70, 71, 75, 78, 101

von Fintel, K. 76, 77, 115

wh-indefinite 16–20